SEEKING HEARTS

LOVE, LUST AND THE SECRETS IN THE ASHES

RYAN GREEN

For Helen, Harvey, Frankie and Dougie

Disclaimer

This book is about real people committing real crimes. The story has been constructed by facts but some of the scenes, dialogue and characters have been fictionalised.

Polite Note to the Reader

This book is written in British English except where fidelity to other languages or accents are appropriate. Some words and phrases may differ from US English.

CONTENTS

True Romance

It was not the easiest time to find a date. The Great War had taken so many of the men, and those that had come home were survivors, they were changed, harsh and broken, all the romance in their hearts burned away by the whistling shells and the blood they had shed. Looking to those few who had been left behind was an even more dangerous proposition given the fact that even criminals had been set loose from prison so that they could join in the battle against the German invaders. The elderly and the infirm had been barred from service, but so too were they removed from the dating pool for the most part. These were not modern times when a woman could marry for love alone and know that she would be able to support herself should the need arise. Times were changing, but they were changing so slowly that to look upon the change as it transpired was akin to watching paint dry. A man needed to be a provider, and the number of independently wealthy men who'd sat out the war, thanks to some existing ailment or by some special dispensation, left slim pickings that only the most beautiful or most well-connected had any hope of snatching up.

These unfortunate circumstances meant that when the time came to seek a husband or even just a lover, French women had to lower their standards somewhat. They had to be willing to overlook certain eccentricities and demurely accept stories riddled with conspicuous holes. They had to look the other way and pretend that the man that held their hand was not telling them any lies when it was blatantly obvious that they were.

To take up with a widower would once have been considered a minor scandal, but now a well-to-do widower was considered a prize catch. A man who had been in good enough shape that another woman had at some time wanted him suggested that there was hope. It meant that they'd likely be a touch older than might have been entirely desirable, but on balance, probably worth the sacrifice.

Added to these challenges were the circumstances of the woman in question. Women with children already kicking around would once have been shunned as the lowest of the low, mothers of bastards, disreputable. The war had created a great many widows, but just as many young girls had given up their virtue to their sweethearts before they went off to battle on the promise that they would be reunited when all was said and done, only to discover that their lover had never returned from the trenches. If there was no father currently in the picture, most people would extend the courtesy of pretending that there had been a marriage somewhere in a girl's past. It provided something of a free pass for a great many of the girls of looser morals who had found themselves in such predicaments before the war began, but it seemed fair to give them that pass so that the many women who had lost their men would not suffer undue indignity.

For La Belle Mythese, such a free pass was her only hope of passing in society. During the war, she had made a name for herself among the soldiers as an entertainer of great renown. Famed across the hospitals from Paris all the way to the Rhine. The exact kind of entertainment that she provided to soldiers had never been made explicit, even when they discussed such matters in later years, but it seems entirely reasonable that whatever minor musical talents she may have displayed in the mess halls would not have resulted in the massive compensation that she received from those who departed the halls with her afterwards.

In her late thirties now, her future was beginning to look bleak. With the war over, she was now only one among a great many "entertainers" at work in Paris rather than the sole available starlet willing to spend time with non-commissioned officers of the French Army, and as such, she had retired into the obscurity of her birth name of Marie Marchadier. She kept a small apartment which was rapidly devouring what was left of her savings, and before long it became apparent that even the squalor in which she now lived was beyond her means. At one time she had dined in the finest restaurants of France and been gently placed upon the finest eiderdowns in the great houses of the country, but now she was forced to post an advertisement in the paper for people willing to buy her furniture.

It was a new low for her, parting with the last measures of finery that she'd been able to carry off with her from one place to the next as she went through her post-war decline. Some of the furniture had been in her family for generations. It was not only her personal fortune that was being passed off so that she might keep food in her belly, but the history of her entire bloodline being brought to so sorrowful an end.

She should have been overwrought and riddled with shame, but shame was something that she had long ago left behind, and the grim emotions borne from having to part with her belongings could be set aside for now. She had always been good at escaping into the safe and warm parts of her mind until moments of discomfort had passed. It had very nearly been the only prerequisite for her career.

As she sat there across from the bald and bearded tradesman who had come to strip her of the last vestiges of a good life, she found to her immense surprise that she had no need to hide from the situation at all. He was soft-spoken and kind in a way that she could not have predicted. Soft in all the ways that men who had been in the war could not have been. He offered his sincere sympathies as readily as his business card and with unexpected gallantry helped her inventory her remaining belongings, evaluating which items would sell for the most and which the least in an effort to leave her with as many of her treasured keepsakes as possible – earning her enough money to sustain her through these hard times.

She could not place the exact moment she knew for certain that he was overpaying her for the furniture. She had imagined that such craftsmanship was in short supply after all the destruction of the war, and that prices may have been driven up by the shortage, but surely there was no way that prices were driven so high on everything. After a moment of doubt, she felt confident that if she were to call up anybody else in Paris for this same assessment, they'd be offering her a fraction of the price.

Once or twice, she proffered an item that she knew was worthless and he found some hidden facet of the design that transformed it into a collectable. He was a blatant liar, but since his lies were clearly of benefit to her, it was difficult to be annoyed about it. Clearly, he wanted to give her money, he wanted to help her out, so why shouldn't she let him? There was no rule in the books that said you had to reject the kindness of strangers. She'd never learned that lesson in church on a Sunday morning. An argument could be made that she'd been relying on the kindness of men to get by for her entire life, if you assumed that her relationships were founded on gifts and companionable revelry rather than on the starkly transactional reality.

But it was that more transactional reality that she had spent the past decade or more living in, and it was with an eye to that version of the world that she began to examine her visitor. He was older than her by a decade or more, but this would hardly be the first time that she had a suitor that she could not have gone to school with. His hair was thinning on the top, beyond thin and all the way too bald in truth, and his beard, while well-kept, was considerably more erratic than she might have liked in a man. Still, there was a warmth to him that she couldn't quite reject, despite his relatively mundane appearance. An almost paternal care for her, and a willingness to set aside business whenever she desired and meander with her down the lanes of memory.

Almost as soon as she had met him, Marie felt as though she could trust him. And after the life that she had lived, that in itself was setting off alarm bells in her head. How could she trust anyone so quickly? Knowing what she knew of the true nature of men, how could she allow one to sit there and lie to her all day long, and take it as a kindness? It was madness to trust a liar, madder still to find excuses for him to linger around, hiding away pieces of furniture that she'd had no intention of showing. Even the secrets of her boudoir were laid out not as a temptation for this stranger, or even as an invitation, but as a sign of her trust. She could count on one hand the number of men that had seen the bedroom in which she slept at night.

Her two pet Brussels Griffon dogs seemed to take to this stranger almost as much as she did, laying their heads upon his lap as the man and woman sat speaking. It was quite uncanny – usually when she had gentleman callers the duo had to be locked in the kitchen to keep them from growling, but they had followed this fellow around as though he smelled like a roast dinner. Marie had caught no such aromas on the gentleman. If anything, he was meticulously devoid of any and all smells. She supposed that a man in the antique trade would have to be careful to avoid the scent of mustiness and assumed that he'd have covered it up with cologne, but all that she could really discern from him was a trace of carbolic soap.

She was not accustomed to the company of a man without a hint of sweat on him. Even when she was not engaged in those activities for which she had become famed, men around her had their eyes fixed on her – they had lewd intentions that rose to the surface in a prickling of salt water. Yet this stranger, for all that he showed intent fascination with her, was not lost to lust the way that she had expected. And it threw her more than she could have anticipated. To have a man show that he cared about her without wanting her carnally? It made no sense to her, and so, like a tongue prodding at a cavity, she kept on extending the time they spent in one another's company, knowing that there would be this discomfort, but going back for more, again and again, all the same.

Before he departed, she had already made arrangements to see him again socially, and he had left her with a deposit on the furniture he meant to buy from her. It might as well have been a gift, for she knew that even if she never parted with a single item he would not demand its return. It was a down payment on time spent together, a cushion that she could rest upon while he tried to conceive of some way that she might get enough money to live without having to part with her heirlooms and such finery as she still clung to.

Although welcome, the money was not what remained at the forefront of her mind, but the other possibilities for the future that had started unfolding before her. If he could be entrapped, if he could be sheltered from the knowledge of who and what she once was, then he might provide her with everything that she desired. A real life, separate from the woman she had been.

The expected transaction never arrived. She kept on waiting for it, for the other shoe to drop, for the mask to fall away and for her new beau to reveal his true nature, but it just did not happen. Either he was truly a decent and kind man behind closed doors or he had suppressed all thoughts and feelings so thoroughly that even in their most intimate moments nothing could break to the surface. And in truth, after a month or more of dinner dates and sweet nothings whispered in her ear, Marie would have welcomed an open-handed slap when she talked back to him, or the whispered request for something she'd have to have charged extra for in her old career.

She almost wanted the beautiful crystalline statue of a perfect future to show its cracks so that it would not be her fault when it was cast down to the ground and shattered. But he just wouldn't do it. He wouldn't be anything less than the ideal suitor, and when the time came that he got down on one knee and proposed to her, never having asked about her past, never having slapped her across the face, never having pushed for anything obscene, she literally had no excuse to say no to him. Why on earth would she turn down exactly what she had been hoping and dreaming about through these long hard months in Paris as everything dried up and she'd lost all she'd loved? To reject him would have been madness, and no matter how her old suspicions reared their ugly heads every time he showed her kindness, she could ignore them. She had to ignore them. She couldn't go on living on bread crusts and charity.

She couldn't go on living in Paris at all, where every so often a man's head would turn as she strolled the boulevards with her dogs, and they would both know that the last time they had met each other had been in some stuffy back room after a performance, where she'd earned her keep and done her part for France to keep the war effort plodding on. Sweat and rough woven uniform fabric rubbing against bare skin. She could almost feel it in their gaze. The heat of the closets where she'd taken them. Where she'd earned her living and her reputation.

La Belle Mythese was dead, Marie had killed her, but everywhere that Marie went the ghost of La Belle was there. At a glance, in a hint of perfume in the air, a whiff of cigarette smoke. She was still being followed by the grand shadow of a wartime madam with every step, and the future that she wanted for herself might have held some trace of that old glamour, but it could not be built on the same foundations. It had to be real, not bought.

So she received the engagement ring, and refused to listen to the gnawing voice at the back of her head warning her that this couldn't be real, that nobody would truly want her after what she had made herself become. Her suitor did not live in Paris, she knew – they stayed in hotels or in her embarrassingly small apartment when they made love. Yet she knew that he owned a home somewhere, the nature of his business would necessitate such a thing, even for the most itinerant of salesmen. So it came as no surprise when he informed her that he had a little chateau out in the country where he would like for the two of them to live together.

Once more, all of this felt like a dream, like something out of a fairy tale, a holiday in Arcadia. Even when she was on the train, with him sitting beside her, holding her hand, she could not quite bring herself to believe it. They would live together in sin for only a short while longer, then there would be a little chapel, a parish priest, and a future like she'd only seen in romance novels. All of the things that she had thought could never come into her life were suddenly right there for the taking, and all that she had to do was resist the urge to spoil it all.

When they arrived, he insisted upon picking her up and carrying her over the threshold, though they were still far from bound in matrimony. There were flowers growing everywhere that she looked, and though the house was small, there was such charm to it as she could scant believe.

To call it a honeymoon would not have been entirely apt, because the arrangements for them to wed had not yet been made, but it felt like one all the same. This change of scenery, this dream of a life being offered up to her on a silver platter. Who was she to complain if the platter was a hand-me-down? What right did she have to resent that there were already women's clothes hanging in the wardrobes of her new changing room, clearly left behind by her widower's former wife?

After only a few short weeks of being happily addled with the romance of her new situation, her suitor left her behind to go back out into the world to conduct his business. She began to feel her predecessor's presence in whichever room of the house she entered. It seemed that the dead woman's ghost followed her everywhere.

They never spoke of the woman that her lover had married before her. Never said her name, or discussed the life that they had lived together, or even mentioned the nature of her demise, but like a detective in one of the novels she so voraciously consumed, she began to piece things together for herself from the evidence that had been left behind.

It must have been some kind of wasting sickness that had taken his first wife. Something that had shrunk her stature over a long period of time. Why else would there have been so many different sizes of dresses hanging in the wardrobe? There were even shoes in different sizes. What must it have been like for that poor woman? To shrink and shrink away to nothing until even your shoes fell from your feet and you could do nothing about it. What a horror.

Worse, though, than the sickness must have been the loneliness. In the city, there had always been someone else around, an overabundance of people, in truth. She had left the city in no small part to break free from the constant pressure she felt as a result of the perpetual judgement she saw in the eyes of others. But out here there was nobody at all – the nearest neighbour was no longer on the other side of a hallway but, rather, a healthy hike away through the nearby woods. At least her dogs were greatly benefiting from all the space to roam free, and they would, no doubt, have loved the long walk through the woods for her to find another person to talk with, but she couldn't quite bring herself to do it.

She was still afraid to show her face, the face which had once drawn crowds and made her famous, for fear that she might be recognized and somebody might tell her new husband of her history. It was not as though she had to walk on eggshells around her beau. He had never demanded any purity of her, never set her on any pedestal, in truth, had never made any sort of demand at all. All that he asked of her was her company, and even of that, he was not overly demanding. The move to the country had been a matter of course, rather than out of his desire to carry her off into the wilderness. She was here by her own choice. He had offered this new life up to her like a gift and she had seized it, the chance to escape, to be free of her ghost.

But her escape was elusive as she was still haunted, doubly haunted now, with the dead wife lingering around every corner and the dead whore lurking in the shadows waiting to pounce. Throughout the long dark hours of the night, both these ghosts swirled around her, scratching at the windows, creaking the wood frame of the house and making her flinch at the sound of voices in the road when dawn finally arrived.

When her suitor came home, it was a beautiful place full of joy and laughter, but when he left – and he always left – the memories returned. The bad times souring the good, the men who hadn't wanted to pay, the ones who'd slapped her around, the pain of pushing through when she never wanted to do it to start with. Picking up sweaty five-franc notes from a bed that was no longer fit for sleep.

It pried at her. Made her old suspicions flare up all over again. Made her go digging despite knowing that there was nothing she could find to make her life better. There were drawers in the antique furniture that were locked, the doors were all open, and the whole house was hers, but there were these odd little crevices that he claimed he didn't have the keys for anymore, that he'd never had the keys for. Something to forget about, yet something that she couldn't let go.

One bad night passed her by, all alone in the cold dark house, with her betrothed off in the city making deals to keep them both in comfort. With dawn she went to the kitchen, digging through the drawers that were open to her in search of some sort of answer. Some way that she could set her worries at ease and convince herself that there was no doom lurking behind the door, just waiting to burst in.

She took up a butter knife and went to work on the closest locked-up desk, jamming it into the crevice between drawer and top, levering up and down, up and down, setting the wood creaking, and splintering the antique varnish away, her wrist aching with the effort. A sharp ping rang out from inside the apparatus as the lock leapt out of place.

There should have been nothing inside, or the belongings of some old owner. Some lost old papers gone yellow with age or a dried-out quill, perhaps. Not letters. Not letters addressed to this chateau, to a man whose name was not her fiancé's but was close enough that it could be considered a pseudonym. Not dozens, no, hundreds of letters from women all over

France, correspondence just like she had sent to him, part business, part flirtation. Lonely hearts columns that he'd replied to. Advertisements for furniture for sale that he'd used to start conversations.

She had not expected him to be a monk before he met her, she knew that she had no moral high ground to stand on, but there was a world of difference between the degree of deception involved in her omission and all of this. She had kept things from him, that was true, but she had not kept something like this. This was not the sign of a healthy mind, this was a sickness, a perversion of the relationship that they had forged. He had not been speaking exclusively to her, he had not been speaking exclusively to any of these women, there were hundreds upon hundreds of different addresses, different letters, different stories that he was spinning. Lies, endless webs of lies to entangle all these different women. What purpose could all of this possibly serve? What was he trying to get out of this? He had only a single home to fill, a single bed to keep warm, what possible reason could he have had for keeping all of these lines in the water? It made no sense.

She crammed all of them back into the drawer. She did her best to smooth the ruptured wood back down. If her suitor looked too closely, her deception would be revealed, but he had never shown very much interest in the furnishings that were supposedly his entire profession. Now that some degree of suspicion had been confirmed, the floodgates of paranoia swung open. What did she actually know about this man? What could she say for certain, that wasn't based on something that he had told her? What did she know, actually know, as absolute fact, about him at all?

He had told her that he had a business, that he had a home, that he was a widower, and that he wanted to spend his life with her, yet here he was corresponding with hundreds of other women with just as much warmth and intimacy as he had shown her. How was she meant to reconcile these two realities? For a day and a night, she could not rest or settle, she fussed with things around the house, trying to set them in some semblance of order, to counterbalance the disorder running rampant in her mind. But now, everything that she had seen and understood became a mystery once more. What if there had been no wife who died? What if there had been no gradual withering? All of the clothes could have been from other women that he'd tricked into this very same situation. Other women who he found when they were vulnerable and preyed upon, inviting them out here to live in sin with him until he grew tired of them. They had not set a date for the wedding, was this why? Had he never meant to marry her at all, just use her for her body and her company until he tired of her and lost interest?

The sinister voice of her past self cursed her for having been so easily taken in. She knew what men were like, why had she deluded herself into believing that this one was any different? She did know what men were like and because of this, genuine fear began to creep in. She had been safe while she believed him, while she trusted in all of his lies, trapped in a little bubble, held away from reality, but now that the bubble had burst, she would no longer be able to go on floating safely by. He was going to realize what she had learned. He was going to turn violent, like men always did when you poked a hole in whatever lie they were telling. All that she'd been hoping for was about to be snatched away, and if she was lucky, she'd get to crawl away with her tail between her legs. She pulled out her suitcase and started filling it up. All the nice clothes that she still clung to like the skin she should have shed. All the presents that he'd showered upon her since she had moved into his home. On the whole, it amounted to next to nothing, especially when compared to what she had lost. Her apartment was gone. Her furniture was gone. She had no money to her name. If she walked away from this place right now, she wouldn't even have sufficient funds to get back to Paris. It would just be her and her two dogs wandering the countryside, sleeping under hedgerows until they all eventually died of starvation.

She looked down into that case full of all her worldly possessions, and she saw the future that she'd been dreaming of. Dresses that didn't have to show anything off, because they were meant to keep her comfortable and safe at home. Costume jewellery that would only be worn for a fancy meal out on the town with her husband. All of the lies of her past are buried. All of the hardships were forgotten. And she had ruined it all by forcing open that drawer.

This didn't have to be the end. She couldn't go back to the way things were before she'd opened Pandora's box, but she didn't have to run. Her fiancé wasn't like the men that she'd known before. He was gentle and kind. He loved her. She knew it in her heart. He did, he loved her. The nipping at her heels by the ghost of her past self could be ignored. Who she used to be would have been running by now, but she didn't want to be that person anymore. She didn't have to jump to conclusions and let paranoia win. She could just talk to him. There was no reason she couldn't just talk to him and let everything go back to the way she wanted it to be. Maybe he had a good reason.

Maybe this was his sales pitch, cosying up to these women so that he could make better deals. Maybe, just maybe, he had dated women before her. Who the hell was she to judge anybody for a checkered past when it came to romance?

She went back to the desk drawer, pulled out all of the letters, and laid them out on the top of the desk. They looked like a lot. They looked like so many letters to so many women, but if they had been spread out over the years and decades since his wife had died, she supposed that they could have been justified. If the clothes that had been hanging in her closet when she arrived had belonged to more than one of her fiancé's past loves, was that really the most terrible truth that could have come out? She kept her past held tightly against her chest, so why wouldn't he hold back the embarrassing truth that he'd been looking for somebody like her for a long time? Looking for love in all the wrong places until she came along.

When he came home, she would tell him what had happened. She would tell him that she had been trying to get some of the stuck drawers open so that they could make use of the furniture. She didn't have to tell him that she went hunting for a reason not to trust him. There would be some degree of confrontation, she could not avoid it, but it did not have to be what her worst fears were telling her it would be. It didn't have to be the end of all this. She just had to find a path down the middle.

It was only as she reached this same conclusion that she heard the griffon hounds barking. Not the aggressive sound they made when they caught sight of a stray cat roaming in the garden, but the excitement that had once been reserved only for the sight of her own return home. Her fiancé must have returned. She'd had no word of his impending arrival or she would have dressed up for the occasion – she was now every bit the country housewife that he had tried to make of her, with none of the glamour that had once been her calling card. The endless pursuit of it no longer interested her, but being able to whip it out, particularly in situations where things might be tense and she needed a man's mind elsewhere, still made things all the easier for her. But of course, with no warning, no time to prepare herself, over-burdened with the weight of all the anxiety she'd spawned from days spent working herself up into a frenzy, she found herself at a loss of how to proceed. He was back and she hadn't a clue what to do. She could hear him walking up the path. There on the desk lay all of the letters, still strewn about, ready to confront him the moment he stepped in the door. An argument in waiting, an argument that might be the end of them. She heard his hand upon the door handle, and she ran. Through the chateau, out into the hall and straight into his arms. He dropped his case, wrapped his arms around her, met her kiss with an ardour that she had never hoped anyone might feel for her, just her, without any affectation.

This was too precious to throw away over a misunderstanding. She would give him every opportunity to explain, she'd believe every lie, anything, so long as she didn't have to give up her hope. Cynicism was for the young, there was not enough time left to live a good life if she didn't believe in what she had, here and now.

Taking him by the hand, she led him through, letting him see what she had done without accusation or apology. He looked at the letters, all of the letters that damned him, and he let out a heavy sigh. The drawer was jammed, or so he had said. He had had no opportunity to clear things out. His expression was enough that she felt an apology would be asking too much, he showed such desolation at the sight of them all, at all the failed attempts to get what he now had with her. It went beyond embarrassment and into some sort of existential dread. For a time she could not place it, but then it snapped into place in her mind. He was afraid that she was going to leave him over this.

Instead, she came up behind him and wrapped her arms around his body. She whispered sweet nothings in his ear, comforting him like she would a child. It was alright. She wasn't going anywhere. He did not need to be ashamed.

He would not look at her, but instead pulled free, gathering all of the letters together and carrying them through to the lounge where the wood-burning stove that warmed the whole chateau stood. He laid them down on a table and turned to stoke up the flames. It was a mild enough day that she had kept only a few logs burned down to a charcoal smouldering, but he piled in wood until there was a blazing inferno within.

Then he turned from it, at last, the same stricken look still upon his face. He was going to pick up the letters, cast them in, and put the past behind him. He was going to explain it all away and everything was going to be fine, and they were going to move on. He need not have stoked the fire so high that she started to sweat, but she could always understand a man's desire for dramatics. Why have an ember when you can have an inferno?

She did not reach for him and try to stop him, because in truth removing those letters from her home would have slain one of the many ghosts that still stalked her. It would have quieted that voice still warning her that this was a mistake, that she should run. If there were no letters, she didn't have to think about what they meant, or what they meant to him. She didn't have to worry that this was all some long con, like La Belle Mythese would have insisted that it was.

But it was not the letters he went to, with that look of desolation, it was her. And she opened her arms and let him step in close and drew him in tight against her in an embrace that she hoped would tell him all that he needed to know. That he was loved, that he was safe, that he had no need to worry about anything at all.

But his hands, they did not find their way around her. His arms were in between their bodies, not wrapped around the outside. They came up between them, brushing up over the length of her body, the way that the men in the dancehalls would sometimes pretend that touch was accidental. They spread as they passed over her chest, drawing a surprised gasp from Marie.

It was the last breath that she would ever take.

His hands closed on her throat. His arms forced her away, forced her down. He rode her body to the carpet, knees on top of her, hands locked tight about her neck. She could not breathe, and she could not understand. Why was he doing this? What was he doing?

She had already forgiven him. She had made sure not to anger him. She had done everything right. There was no reason for him to turn on her. For a moment, in her shock, she did not even fight back. When the men she'd whored for turned violent, she had always been ready, but like the fool she'd made herself, this time she had been so sure that the man was good that she wasn't prepared to protect herself. Lo and behold, he was a man like all of the other men. A monster like all the rest. A beast, dressed in a suit, the better to stalk its prey.

By the time she got her hands on his wrists and started pulling them away, digging in her nails, trying so desperately to save herself, she was too weak to make him move. As she weakened, he seemed to grow more and more powerful with every passing moment, dragging her across the floor like a rag doll. Her mild-mannered antique dealer of a husband-to-be was throwing her around like she was a tiny mouse, and he a cat.

The dogs came tearing into the room then, and she thought that she was saved, that they would leap to her aid. But he had bought them with table scraps and walks in the countryside, he'd won them away from her without her even knowing. The dogs bounced and bounded all around them as they lay there on the floor. Barking and barking until her whole world was nothing but a wall of that noise and the ringing in her ears. At some point, they upended the table that held all the letters causing them to rain down on her even as her vision faded.

She should have left the locked drawer closed. She should not have looked the gift horse in the mouth. All her regrets echoed in her mind as she sank into darkness.

Then she was gone, and the fire awaited.

Altar Boy

On the 12th of April 1869, Henri Désiré Landru was born in Paris. His father was a furnace stoker, who spoke little and worked a great deal, while his mother ran a laundry service from their home, later ably assisted by her eldest daughter, then little more than a toddler.

The family were devout Catholics, or at least his parents were, and they intended to instil the same values in their son. Henri, however, was less inclined to blind faith and manual labour than his parents. His was a mind that seemed to constantly be spinning with new thoughts and ideas that would not have occurred to either parent if they had been given a hundred years. They recognised that spark of intelligence in him early in life and endeavoured to make certain it flourished, spending what little they could spare to buy the boy books, and promising his sister, when she was deprived of dolls and toys, that it would all be worth it at the end when her brother would make his fortune and care for them all.

In light of his burgeoning intellect, the Landru parents seemed to become even more devoted to their faith, praising God for the gift that had been bestowed upon their son who they knew would someday be a genius and change the world. But not every part of that newfound fervour was necessarily bereft of ulterior motives. They travelled every day to the Ile Saint-Louis, a little island on the Seine that had been given over almost entirely to the church, and there they worshipped in a very specific church. A church where the boy was rapidly conscripted into being an altar boy and assisting around the place as much as possible to ingratiate himself with the clergy. Even at so young an age, Henri was able to grasp that there was a purpose to these interactions, and he was not simply being handed over to serve the church without any reason. As such, he was more than diligent in his duties, becoming a favourite of the priests that worked there and the monks who did their work in the adjacent building.

When Henri was old enough to attend, he was readily accepted into the school where those monks taught. He had put in the time and the work, and his parents did their best to ensure his acceptance by tithing every penny they could afford.

He thrived in the structured environment of the school, obeying to the letter every rule laid out, avoiding all temptations to misbehave or wander astray like so many of his peers. He was focused upon the education that he could receive there, and the potential doors that it would open for him later in life. Mathematics and practical work were his preference, and he was a competent woodworker, with dreams of advancing to metalwork before he reached his teenage years.

Continuing his service within the church to maintain the good graces of the clergy who were essentially funding his education, Henri graduated from being an altar boy to being a fully-fledged sub-deacon. It was a secular post that involved helping the priests into their holy vestments, lighting candles around the building and generally lending a hand wherever it was needed. He applied the practical skills that he had learned in school wherever possible, conducting minor repairs about the church, and even assisting the priests in counting out the money brought in via the donation platters each Sunday. This was well beyond what could have been expected of any sub-deacon of his age, but his competence and good nature were well known to all, and he had earned their respect despite his humble beginnings.

His parents, of course, could not have been more pleased. Everything that they had hoped that Henri might achieve in his life seemed to be coming together for him, and he began to speak of his future in more certain terms. Not as idle daydreams, like so many of his fellow students, but with the certainty of a young man who was beginning to develop a plan. He had an interest in engineering, he had borne witness to some of the wonders that this new world offered over the past few years, and he was thrilled at the possibilities new machines could offer to mankind. It was his intention to work primarily in engineering, but to make his fortune as an inventor, designing and creating new machines for a variety of purposes, with an emphasis on the growing field of transportation.

Cars, motorbikes, and the like all fascinated the boy, and through the church congregation, he was able to get hands-on experience with a few of these ingenious new devices. It was as though the quiet and well-mannered boy was entirely transformed in their presence, excitement bubbling over. He became giddy, the way you'd expect of a child, but giddy over new understandings that he'd reached. Other little boys might have looked upon a motorbike and been excited by the prospect of going fast – he was excited to learn how the spark plugs ignited the gas fumes.

In any other child, claims that he would become a great inventor would have been dismissed as fantasy, but Henri showed all the signs of being able to carry through on his dreams and delivering realities.

Yet academia was never going to be a possibility for a child coming from a family of such modest means. When his schooling, courtesy of the church came to an end, he was left without any real means to pursue his dreams, at least for the time being. His father interceded by speaking with his own employers at the Vulcain Ironworks to see if it would be possible for the boy to receive some sort of apprenticeship. He asserted that the boy's talents with machinery would be a great benefit to the place, but in those days there was little automation involved in the craft. Almost everything was done by the strength of hand and winch, far harder to manage than simply relying upon technology. He was brought in to look over their furnaces and make any suggestions that he could, but there was little room for improvement on such basic and antiquated technologies. There would be no job for him following in his father's footsteps. The boy could not have become a stoker like his father, because he lacked the physicality for such a role. He may have been clever, but he was neither tall nor well-muscled, and his stamina could not have held up to the relentless backbreaking work that would have been required of him.

But once more, the community and the church pulled through for the devout boy. With a bequest from the church, funded by a whip-round among the congregation, he was able to undertake a few classes in his seventeenth year of age at the prestigious Paris School of Mechanical Engineering. Nowhere near enough for any sort of qualification, but enough to give him a grounding in the work that he hoped someday to pursue. He excelled in those classes, impressing his tutors with his intelligence and hardworking nature, but the charity that would have been required to further his education was not forthcoming. The church had already given him a great deal in exchange for his dutiful service. The cost of fully educating him beyond that point was simply beyond the means of the congregation.

With the knowledge that he had acquired, he was able to find some part-time work in an automobile garage. Setting himself apart from his colleagues and the apprentices to the trade who could all troubleshoot common problems they encountered, Henri had an obvious in-depth understanding of how the mechanical make-up of cars actually worked. It seemed clear to everyone that he was going to go far in the business, but before that, he had some other duties that he needed to contend with.

At eighteen years, all boys who were physically able were conscripted to serve in the French army. Henri was no exception, and he did not cower at the prospect. If anything, he was relatively excited about the potential opportunities that might arise. Mechanised warfare was still in its infancy, but if his aptitude was taken into account, he might have had the opportunity to work on the kind of heavy-duty equipment that he never encountered in the garage. The prospect of working with tanks, however, was not the only source of excitement in young Henri's life.

From early adolescence, Henri had developed an avid interest in the fairer sex, choosing to spend time in the company of women as much as possible and coming quite close to neglecting his other responsibilities as a result of his intense focus on romancing the ladies. His luck was inconsistent at best, in no small part due to the fact that his dating pool consisted almost exclusively of conservative Catholic girls. Even with this limitation, however, it seemed that the boy's ability to woo the ladies was not to be underestimated – as evidenced by a scandalous pregnancy scare involving one of his cousins. This distressing incident had him skating on thin ice in his role as sub-deacon for quite a few months.

Henri would find love again, and all too quickly, in the months before his conscription. Marie-Catherine Remy first laid eyes upon Henri during mass one evening, and she was immediately taken with him. His bushy eyebrows and thick hair gave him the look of something of a wild man, but the piercing intellect shining out from behind his spectacles was what really pinned her to the spot when their gazes finally met. This was a man who could look at her and understand her entirely, nothing like the boors that had tried to court her thus far. He would listen while she spoke, and understand what she was trying to tell him, instead of hearing only what he wanted to hear. This was the kind of boy who she could see herself marrying one day.

For Henri's part, he needed only to know that there was attention available to him from a woman for him to be immediately invested. It was true that he developed a real affection for Marie-Catherine with time, and that their fledgling romance blossomed into something so much greater, but the sad fact of the matter was that if any girl in that congregation had turned lustful eyes upon him, he would have been there in an instant.

He met up with her after mass had ended and offered to walk her home, taking the scenic route along the riverside. It was quite late, and dark, and her family were all standing there staring at her as she listened to his invitation, but she could not bring herself to say no to him. Not when he made it so abundantly clear that she was not alone in her longing for company and affection. She had seen him and wanted him for what he was, and he had done the same. For teenagers on the precipice of adulthood, confused and off balance, that was the kind of solid foundation that anything could have been built upon.

So they walked, and they talked, and he made his intentions towards her clear. This was not a friendly discussion she reckoned but a courtship that he meant to commit himself to. There was a maturity about him that she found both shocking and refreshing when placed in comparison to her previous attempts at dating. An intensity of attention that made her feel special, as though he could have been turning all of that burning intellect to anything in the world but had chosen her, and her alone, to be its recipient. It was difficult not to feel some degree of flattery at that. For all that he was still short in stature, and obviously young, he spoke about things as though he were a grown man. When the conversation turned to the future, he really shone, speaking of his education, and the plans that he was making for a better future not only for himself but for all of mankind. The machines that he would make and how they could change the world. She believed everything that he said, his promise to become wealthy and successful despite his humble beginnings, and in her mind she began to weave herself into that story. She saw herself at his side as he made his great advances, keeping house instead of having to work all hours that God sent, raising his children, and living a life of luxury beyond anything she could have dreamed of for herself.

When the conversation turned back to the present, he made it clear that it was his dream to share it all with her in just the way that she had been imagining. They would be together in the world that he would make if she would have him, and he meant to do everything right to ensure that she understood how seriously he took this matter.

He meant to step out with her, to introduce himself to her parents, to do all of the dutiful things that a young man in their community was meant to do before beginning his pursuit, and she found his old-fashioned good manners to be quite charming. Even when they made it to the door of her home and she dithered for a moment instead of going inside, he did not push his luck and try to kiss her. Or at least, he did not try to kiss her as she might have expected. Instead, he seized her hands between his and brought them up to his lips.

It was another old-fashioned gesture that should have been laughable, as though she were some princess and he a cavalier. An affectation from a fairy tale with no place in the modern world, but when he looked up at her, his lips pressed to her skin and a hunger in his eyes, she understood why this had once set hearts aflame. That the restraint that he was showing was not a lack of passion, but merely a delay of it. A promise of things to come. She could feel her heart hammering within her chest and a blush spreading up her neck. She blessed the night for its darkness, hiding the worst of it, but even so, she had to pluck her hand free and scamper into the house as quickly as she could, only to run, still blushing, directly into the judgmental stares of her entire family who had been anxiously awaiting her return.

The following day, true to his word, Henri called upon her father to ask permission to court her, and to Marie's surprise and delight, he was given the answer of yes. She had thought for certain that her stick-in-the-mud family were going to stand in the way of the first great romance of her life, but it seemed that her father, too, saw the possibilities in Henri. The fact that he had approached them in such a respectful manner and made promises with regard to his treatment of her and the scheduling of their dates had so impressed her father that he didn't even insist on her taking along one of her sisters as a chaperone. Apparently, he trusted Henri to maintain her virtue.

He should have been more concerned with his own daughter's desires than those of this boy, because within moments of their first day "stepping out" together, she was kissing him on the banks of the Seine. As much as Henri attempted to keep her at arm's length and maintain the pretence that he meant only to judge their future plans for marriage upon the value of her companionship and conversation, she would not be deterred. By the time of their third day out together, he had to take some portion of his hard-earned savings and rent out a hotel room, for fear that she might simply mount him on a park bench. The more that he resisted her advances, the more desperate she seemed to become for him. Each kiss that she had stolen had felt like a little victory, and each victory intensified her resolve to push for more and more. To break his composure, to see him sweat and blush the way that he made her.

Yet even in that rented room on a seedy street, with sunlight filtering through the hastily drawn curtains, there was no hint of shame on his face, no blush, no aversion of the eyes. He stared into her soul as she undid her buttons, and while his eyes raked down every inch of her bare skin as it was exposed, it was as though he were observing some interesting machine that he couldn't wait to work with. There was desire there, but none of the wonderment that she herself felt as he pressed his gentle kisses to her skin, and those strong and calloused hands caressed her flesh. He was doing something that he loved, something that he wanted to do all the time, but there was nothing more to it than that. There was no transcendence for him. This was not the most important moment in his life. It was not the fulcrum on which his fate would hinge. But for her, it was everything. It soon became apparent that Henri was not as virginal as she and, despite a fleeting hint of disappointment, she found she was immensely grateful for that as it placed the burden of knowing what should be done in his hands rather than in hers.

They made love often in those early days, burning through his money at hotels, sneaking into their homes when everyone else was out, taking every opportunity to sink into the comfort of one another while trying hard to ignore the anxiety that followed their illicit couplings. If anyone found out what Marie had been doing, her reputation would be destroyed. If Henri wouldn't marry her under such circumstances, she would be doomed to destitution and excommunication from the conservative circles in which her family and Henri's lived. But Marie had no real fear in her heart beyond that of being discovered and kept away from Henri. She knew with all certainty that Henri would marry her, because he loved her, just as she loved him. They were meant to be together for the rest of their lives. To walk down the aisle, raise children, make a home, and grow old and grey in each other's endless companionship.

What else could this longing for him mean if not love? This burning passion consumed her, day and night, to be with him every moment that she could. She was a good girl, raised right, so whatever she was feeling must be love. Lust was an abstract that she had never encountered in real life, a sin born of a poisoned heart that afflicted the grotesque. What she felt was different. Holy.

It had to be, because she was the one feeling it, and there was nothing evil or wrong about it. Yet for all her certainty and all of Henri's promises, they knew that soon they would be divided. Much as he wanted to stay with her, the law would soon intervene and if he did not go willingly to do his service, then he would face jail and contempt. He had to go, but on his return, he would make her his wife. They would be together forever, just as soon as his military service was over. He'd get himself a job and she'd do laundry work for the big houses uptown. They'd work hard and make ends meet until his big dreams for the future came to fruition. Then they could have babies and live in one of those big houses themselves. All of their wildest dreams could come true because she believed in Henri and what he was capable of.

They came together all the more frequently in the days leading up to his departure. Marie became a fixture in the Landru household, essentially adopted ahead of the marriage that everyone now felt was inevitable. In truth, Henri probably would have been equally welcome in the Remy household, despite his lack of refinement, but the young couple chose to stay in the vicinity of his family home because everyone within it was more often occupied and they could sneak off to find a bed together without danger of discovery.

When he took the train to Saint Quentin to begin his three years of service, she was standing there on the platform alongside all the other wives and girlfriends, a sense of sorrow mixed with camaraderie and hope for a brighter future. Henri's father had not been able to get the time off work to see his son depart, but his mother and sister were there, arms wrapped around Marie to keep her steady as the train began to pull away.

They stood there on the platform until the train was out of sight and walked out of the station arm in arm. Henri's mother set off to the market as his sister and girlfriend dawdled along, Marie uncharacteristically quiet. Finally, she gathered her courage and asked the girl that she hoped would someday be her sister-in-law, "How do you know when a woman is pregnant?"

Happy Ever After

She had chosen her confidante well, as it turned out. Henri's sister helped her through the process of doctor's visits and blood tests and all of the rest, and when it began to become more and more apparent that she was with a child, the whole Landru family rallied around her. She could go to her own parents and tell them the truth, knowing that just on the other side of the door, there was a family who would not let the worst happen to her. She would not live in comfort as she had with her own kin, but there would be no homelessness or starvation in her future. No nunnery or worse.

Her parents took it surprisingly well, all things considered. They insisted, of course, that she marry Henri, something she had been wanting to do anyway, more or less since the moment she met him.

Henri was of course informed of his new status as the soon-to-be father of a bastard child long before said child's arrival. While he could not immediately return home, the moment that he had an opportunity for leave he was on the train back to Paris, bursting with stories of the army, the work that he was doing there, and his excitement to be marrying so wonderful a woman as the one he'd accidentally impregnated. All seemed to be entirely above board, and there was a general consensus among the families and the congregation that the matter was going to be settled in due time. The wages that Henri was making from his national service were being directed to his bride-to-be, as was right and proper, and while poor Marie suffered through a great many snide comments and dirty looks each time she attended mass, the priests of Ile Saint-Louis chose not to make an example of her. As Jesus had loved Mary Magdalene, so could the conservative Catholics of Paris learn to love young Marie. In truth, she was very easy for them to love, chagrined about the foolishness of giving her virtue away to the first boy that came along, but not ashamed, because it was true love, and they were going to have a future together. Something that was proven time and time again, with each of Henri's visits.

He was not present for the birth of his first child, still serving at Saint Quentin, but at the earliest opportunity, he requested leave and was surprised to find it granted. Despite the ignoble nature of the baby's birth, their newborn daughter, also named Marie, was loved and cared for by both parents and the respective families behind them. Both Maries remained living at the elder's family home, receiving all of the support that she could have hoped for, in addition to frequent visits from the Landru family, bearing such gifts as they had been able to afford. They need not have bothered with such things. The money that Henri was sending back was more than enough to not only keep Marie and the baby in comfort but enough to begin saving for the home they meant to buy when his service was over and they were finally wed.

There was more good news on that front. While there had been no place for Henri in the mechanised corps where he had hoped to find a station, he had soon discovered that his head for numbers and organisational skills were desperately needed in the army, and he had seen rapid promotion to deputy quartermaster with a promise of further promotions if he elected to extend his service beyond the obligatory period. The responsibility was greater, but so too was the compensation, and before long the money required to put down a deposit on a home in Paris was already squared away, and their future looked bright. Henri made frequent use of his leave time to come home and visit with his girlfriend and daughter during this period, resulting in a second pregnancy before marriage as he headed into his third year of military service.

Were it not for that second child, it is possible that Henri would have stayed on in the army, continued rising through the ranks based on his intelligence, and likely would have ended up somewhere in the upper command structure. His morals, however, would not allow him to leave his two children behind, or leave poor Marie to care for both of them on her own.

Nobody back in Paris ever doubted him. They never questioned his loyalty or devotion to the new family that he had started. He had always been such a good boy, so dedicated to doing the right thing. Even if he had allowed his lust to get the better of him once or twice, there was no way that he'd just abandon some poor girl after knocking her up.

They should have questioned his loyalty, and if they had seen how he behaved when he was off in Saint Quentin they would have been shocked and appalled. Around every military base throughout history, there have been women of a certain disposition, interested in the young and attractive men who were serving their country. Some of them belonged to the world's oldest profession, others were simply drawn to the uniform and the scarcity of competition. While other men on campus maintained their dignity and good reputation, Henri had always been a skirt chaser, and neither military enlistment nor fathering children with a girl back home had done anything to dissuade him from pursuing every woman that he encountered. It was a small wonder that he had not been put out of the army on medical grounds, but it seemed that venereal disease, like most other consequences for his actions, would entirely pass Henri by. His brothers-in-arms would forever keep his secrets, just as he would keep theirs. The officers looked the other way, hoping that Henri wouldn't bring shame on the uniform with the way that he was carrying on but were unwilling to discipline him, as that would require acknowledging exactly what the filthy little creature was up to on his nights off.

There was only a little time left for Henri to serve, and the officers were betting heavily that he would escape from the army before any consequences caught up to him, thus alleviating any need on their part to intervene. It seemed that everyone was fortunate in that regard.

Henri's second child, a boy named Maurice would be born shortly before his service was over, and he requested special dispensation at that point to end his service and go home to marry his sweetheart. The dispensation was grudgingly given.

It was not as though France was at war, so the officers had no good reason to deny the young man his return to civilian life a few months early, not to mention that it freed them of the worries of having the young lothario amidst their ranks.

Yet despite his wandering eyes and wandering hands, Henri was true to his promises. He married Marie at the church where they had first met on the Ile Saint-Louis within days of returning to Paris, as soon as the arrangements could be made and the newborn baby parted from her.

It was hardly the social event of the season, but despite the shame that accompanied the specific circumstances of the wedding, there was also sufficient relief in the hearts of all parties involved that both families attended to watch the union being made in the eyes of the Lord and the law.

The tension that had been hanging over both the Remy and Landru households finally gave way, and the last vestiges of hostility that both sides had been clinging to in case of emergency were finally set aside. All was going to be well at last. The young ones were married, they had money enough to start a life together, they had two beautiful, healthy children, and would in all likelihood have considerably more, given how productive they'd been so far. Everything that their families could have wanted for them was coming true. Finally.

They rented an apartment while Henri settled back into civilian life, not ready to buy a house until they knew where his career was going to take him. The endless possibilities of his youth were still there, now reinforced by the experience that he had gained in the fields which were of interest to him, and all that he had to do was make a decision about which of them he wanted to pursue.

While he had profoundly enjoyed the physical work involved in being a car engineer, there were not nearly as many jobs available in that field as there were graduates seeking to enter it, and he had not half of the qualifications that they had – at least, not on paper. More importantly, after his time in the army, it had become apparent to Henri that his body was fallible. He had lacked the strength and stamina to keep up with some of the beefier young men that he had served with, with the net result of him often being punished during their training for failure to maintain a healthy level of competition. Yet when it came time to do the work of the mind, he had left them all behind instantly. While they were still dithering over simple mathematics, he was creating formulas to solve all problems of the same type. The mind was his area of expertise, so working exclusively with his mind was how he meant to proceed. It was his greatest strength, so it made sense to exploit it.

He sought out work as a clerk, first and foremost, a job where his abilities in the field of organisation and fast thinking would be the most beneficial, while still leaving him ample time and energy for activities outside of work so he could pursue his dreams of becoming an inventor.

It did not take long for him to find precisely the kind of work that he wanted, and he was more than willing to put up the bond money required to receive his training there. Paying bond money to an employer was, at that time, a common practice used to ensure that those that a company brought on and trained wouldn't immediately abandon their post and go into work as a competitor. It should have been the start of a brand new life for Henri and his little family, but instead, he encountered the darker side of life for the very first time.

As his employer had requested, he dressed himself formally and then presented himself, first thing on a Monday morning, at their offices. The door was locked, but he had come early to make a good first impression so he did not think twice about it. Then an hour passed. He climbed up onto a windowsill and peered inside, only to discover an empty room, coated in dust. He must have come to the wrong address; he roamed about hunting for the correct one to no avail. Another hour passed, and he went to the local police station to enquire as to the address of the clerk's office in question. It was only when he gave a description of the gentleman who had interviewed him that understanding seemed to dawn upon the faces of the officers he was discussing the matter with. There was no job. There was no office. It had all been a scam. The bond money that he had put up was gone, and he would never see it again. It was not an insubstantial amount of money. Certainly, more than he could raise again any time soon. This meant that the vast majority of middle-class jobs that he had been hoping to segue into after his military career were no longer going to be available to him. In addition to protecting the employers from staff who might run away and make themselves competitors, the system of bonds also prevented the poor and working class from escaping the drudgery of their working lives into comfortable jobs meant for more respectable people. All of the money that he had saved up from his time in the army was gone, overnight. The future he'd been working so hard to secure, gone. All of the possibilities of bringing his dreams to fruition, snatched away from him by a common con man.

Henri had never encountered a situation like this before. All his life, he had done what was required of him, he had done what he had been told was the right thing to do. There was a straightforward path towards his goals, and he had trudged along it, no matter how unsavoury or difficult he may have found it because, in the end, he knew he would receive his just reward. It was the way that the world was supposed to work.

For all that he had been raised Catholic, he had no real belief in the existence of any higher power. He had toed the line and obeyed the strictures because he knew that it paid for him to do so. As long as he did what was asked of him, he would be rewarded for his actions. He might not have had any faith in the Heavenly Father above, but he had faith in the basic transactional nature of society. Good behaviour went in; rewards came out. It was so simple a dog could understand it, and he had never been able to grasp why other people wouldn't follow the same rule to ensure their lives went well. Now he understood.

Now he understood that sometimes you could do everything right and still lose. Now he understood that there was no justice in the world, no balance, only people trying to get what they wanted from one another and using laws and rules as snares to get others to play fair while they cheated. He had done the right thing, he had come home and married the girl, raised the kids, and saved up every penny so he could get a decent start in life, and this was how the world repaid his efforts.

Everything that he had wanted was now out of reach, the life that he had promised Marie had been snatched from her. She had to start working as a laundress, just as his own mother had. Carbolic soap leaving her once soft hands red and rough. The long hours leaving her exhausted and miserable. Eyes watering all the time from the rising steam, tainted with bleach. She had been young and beautiful, unlike any grown woman he had ever known, but now reality was starting to seep in. The harsh life of the working poor took its toll on her day by day, ageing her before her time. Ageing her before his eyes. Stealing everything about her that he'd craved and liked. As for him, his life went from being a bright beacon of excitement and progress to being a cavalcade of dead-ends and failures. He would take up a job that he had little interest in and was more than qualified for, then hold onto it for as long as he could, even though he had little to no enthusiasm for it. But time and time again, his employers went under.

He was brought in by a plumbing firm to handle all of their accounts, and over the course of several months discovered that the business had been running at a loss for years and was on the verge of collapse, but the previous owners had been so bad at accounting that this fact had passed them by. They had to shutter their business after years of what they had considered booming success after Henri's intervention, and there was a great deal of ill feeling about it from everyone involved, none more so than Henri who was being treated like a villain for pointing out the reality that they were facing.

Next, he worked as the "leg-man" for a furniture salesman. Initially, the plan had been to bring him in to do the books, make repairs and generally manage the back end of the business, but it soon became clear to his new employer that Henri was not only charismatic enough to win customers over, he was also smart enough to assess the value of things at a glance, and amoral enough that he had no compunctions about lying to the customers about the value of their belongings if it meant that he could get a better deal for the company. He did exceptionally well in the business, impressing his employer at every turn, but after a brief downturn in sales revenues, he was let go. His employer assumed that anyone amoral enough to trick old ladies out of their heirlooms would not be above pocketing the difference in profits between what was to be expected and what he'd been successfully generating with the sweat of his own brow.

Henri had not been defrauding his employer, there had simply been a brief downturn, but he was personally offended at being accused of such a thing, and once more he found himself leaving employment with a sour taste in his mouth and little to no savings that could have been put towards another bond for employment somewhere else.

Once again, the burden of keeping the family afloat fell to Marie and her clothes-scrubbing abilities. Something that she bore with surprising dignity and grace, never complaining about their circumstances or the greatly lowered expectations for what her life was meant to be. Perhaps she realized that Henri had inadvertently inflicted this upon her by being tricked out of their savings.

The Landru family continued to weigh in, in a manner which was quite surprising to Marie. They would drop in with food, offer to help care for the kids so that she could focus on her work without them underfoot. To her surprise, even the stern-faced patriarch would come by when he wasn't in the metalworks and sit with the children bouncing them on his knee, chattering away to them about nothing in a manner completely contrary to his usual gruff and silent demeanour. He and Marie actually formed something of a friendship, to the surprise of both of them. Neither one was like anyone the other had ever met before, and there was a divide between them of more than just a generational difference, but nonetheless, if asked about her friends, Marie would most likely have included her father-in-law among their number.

The family continued to grow apace, despite Henri's declining affection for his wife becoming increasingly obvious. Another daughter, Suzanne was born in 1896, just after Henri had lost his job with the furniture sales company. Being unemployed, he had some time at home with his newborn and the other children. He even humbled himself to the point of assisting with some of the laundry work, though to anyone who may have looked in and seen the little man in his suit sloshing suds around, the incongruous sight would likely have seemed quite hilarious.

It was about then that Henri came upon the first real opportunity that he had seen in years. There was a toymaker in Paris looking for an assistant. It may not have been the high-stakes engineering work that he had imagined himself undertaking, but it was at least a step in the right direction. He would have the opportunity to do some work in the field of engineering, at least to some degree. He'd be working with the intricate mechanisms of moving toys that were all the rage. The pay was not good, even in comparison to the rather terrible jobs that he had worked in the past, but the possibilities that this role offered up were sufficient for Henri to set that aside. This was a trade he could learn and then work at for the rest of his life if he so chose. It was a step towards making the inventions that he'd dreamed up as a child. His wife would simply have to wash clothes for a few days a week, his children would simply have to make do without bread every so often, and they would all make sacrifices now that would pay off later. That had always been the deal. That had been the deal that the world made with him. He worked hard. He toed the line. Everything paid off.

Yet inside of him, there were no doubts, whispers that tomorrow might never come, that the promises he was making might be proven lies as soon as the wool was tugged from his eyes or the rug pulled out from under his feet. The world did not work like he had been told it would. The promises that his father had made were false, and he did not want to repeat that pattern with his own children. They deserved better than this, and his adherence to the same old game plan was hurting them. He was smarter than everyone that he met, so why was it wrong for him to outsmart them and get what he wanted? If that wasn't the way the world was meant to be, wouldn't he have been born as dumb as his father? Wouldn't his savings still have been his?

The work as an assistant to a toymaker was less than riveting. It included the kind of tasks that would have been handled by vast automatic machinery in just a few years but was still the domain of artisans at this point. Whatever career he might have imagined himself building was going to be wiped away by the relentless grind of progress. He had foresight enough to understand that early, so he began making more profitable use of the time that he had in the workshop. He still completed every task that was set for him in record time, but he did not stop there. With all the tools and supplies available to him, he began to tinker and experiment. Laying out plans for his own automatic toys, for a motorbike, for a car. Building himself prototypes on his employer's tab.

In a normal workplace, this would, of course, have been discovered rapidly, but Henri had been placed in charge of balancing the books almost as soon as he had arrived, and this time around, already had a black mark on his reputation from his previous employer for *false* claims about his character, he felt entirely justified in siphoning off a little money here and there from his new employer to ensure that this was not just another short and useless stint in another dead-end job.

It was a funny thing – if he had just been stealing money like any normal person, he likely would have been caught by his vigilant employer almost immediately, but because he was instead investing the company's money into raw materials and tools, it passed completely unseen. By the time he did eventually part ways with his new employer, having finally recognised that the man never had any intention of actually teaching him anything, and was instead using him for manual labour, Henri had designs, plans, and working mechanisms for a half dozen new projects that he meant to pursue.

Employment was for fools in the opinion of Henri Landru. You would work and work to line another man's pockets and never see a penny of the profit for yourself. His own father was that kind of fool, heading into the Vulcain Ironworks every day of his adult life to shovel coal. Backbreaking labour rewarded with a pittance, and no prospect of advancement anywhere to be seen.

Instead of seeking out a new employer after leaving the toymaker, he began work on building his own business empire. There were three pillars that he meant to build that empire around, and they would remain more or less constant as the years rolled by. Firstly, there was the used furniture business. This was his least profitable enterprise, but also the one that required the least investment. He would visit people who wanted to be rid of furniture and offer them a price for their items, which they could choose to accept, netting him the products he would then sell on to antique traders or thrift stores for a reasonable profit margin, or they would refuse, in which case his only loss would be the time that he had spent talking with them. This also provided him with the opportunity to network with people in the upper classes, as they were the only ones liable to have furniture that had any sort of resale value to speak of. Typically his customers had fallen on hard times themselves if they had been driven to sell their belongings, but that did not mean that their social circles were similarly bereft, and in exchange for offering a more than fair price on certain items and cutting into his profit margins, he could often ingratiate himself sufficiently to earn a decent social standing in those circles. Something that would come in incredibly useful for the other pillars of his empire.

With the money that he had accrued from his furniture sales, Henri invested in a small property. During his off hours, he worked tirelessly at converting it into a garage. When his upper-class friends needed their cars tuned up, they now knew a guy who could do that for them. Many of his old army buddies from the mechanised corps that he'd been cosying up to the whole time that he was serving had taken jobs as drivers for companies in the city. When they encountered mechanical issues that their army training couldn't touch, they knew just who to turn to. Even the Ironworks that had treated his father so harshly throughout the years became a client of the Landru garage, and his reputation soon preceded him whenever he went to meet up with potential new clients. Everything was starting to go his way now that he had turned his incredible intellect towards the goal of making as much money as possible. His family were taken care of properly, they were able to move into accommodations more suited to their increased size, and once more he had begun to claw his way back towards his dreams.

If anything, those dreams of being an inventor were closer than ever before. He had become well known for his skills as a mechanic in all the circles where such things mattered, his genius, such as had been displayed thus far, had been lauded by everyone involved. His parents were finally able to point to their son at mass and proudly declare his accomplishments. The time had never been better for him to strike while the iron was hot and invent something entirely new.

And so the third pillar of his business empire was constructed: Invention. In 1898, he unveiled the prototype of the first of what he meant to be a great many new products. A new design of motorbike that he casually named the Landru.

Motorbikes had existed before this point, of course, and they had even seen use by the army, but the price point attached to them had left them inaccessible to the general public, even though they would have provided the maximum amount of societal good to middle-class workers in cities. Henri's plan was to change all of that. Using lower-cost materials in novel ways, he meant to mass produce his Landrus and sell them at a far lower price point than motorbikes currently on the market. Increasing accessibility and bringing hundreds, if not thousands of new clients into the market for his garage, while simultaneously boosting the reputation of that garage through the amazing workmanship that went into every machine.

The main problem with this plan was that the less expensive materials weren't already being used in novel ways to produce motorbikes cheaply because they didn't work. The prototype would run, of course, and he could show it off to anyone interested, but in the long term, the machines lacked sustainability. The cheaper parts would break, almost without warning, when put under the stress of regular use. Henri was working on his prototype in the garage almost every day, tweaking and replacing parts with more expensive ones that would actually do the job. If it had been released onto the market in its current form, he would have been looking at massive outcry and likely bankruptcy as people were injured by the failing machines. By the time he was finished with his prototype, it had cost many times the price tag of the usual motorbike and he'd ended up using almost all of the same materials as the ones already on the market, assembled piecemeal as one fault after another developed. Much of those costs were due to him having to fabricate the same parts over and over again with increasingly expensive materials, and in small batches, but even if he were to take his final product and put it into production, all that he was left with was a motorbike that cut a few corners to shave a few francs off the price tag instead of the revolution in transportation that he had been aiming for.

His first grand design was a failure. His innovation had ended up leading him back to exactly the same point that all of his existing competitors had already come to, and even with the reduction in costs that mass production would allow him, he was going to end up either selling the Landru at no profit or selling it at the same price point as his already established competitors.

If he had been quietly working on this project in isolation, this would have been the point when it should have been abandoned. Filed as a failure, put onto a shelf, and forgotten about until technology had advanced a little further, allowing new cheaper materials to fulfil the role he had outlined for them. Decades down the line, what Landru had been trying to achieve became the norm as fibreglass bodies and cheaper methods of metal casting came about, but in the present, where Henri resided, the project could not proceed.

Except that it had to. Henri had not been quiet about his big idea. He had been showing off his prototype since the moment he had first gotten it running, and building up hype about the project with the intention of snaring himself a few investors from the upper crust who could benefit from his grandiose business plan. Things were already in motion, and if he were to back down now, he would lose not only his face but also the reputation that he had been building in these circles. He could not afford that. So despite the flaws in his designs, he was forced to carry on.

As the only one involved in the business with sufficient technical know-how to understand the failure, he was able to keep it entirely under wraps. And when the investors began approaching him, instead of him having to chase them, he had no choice but to take the money that was being offered to him. Every night, when his working day was done, he would sequester himself in the workshop, banging his head against his unsolvable problem. Not only the problem of the machine itself but the larger apparatus that now had been attached to the machine, the various investors who were growing increasingly impatient to see his factory built and their stake in the business paying out. It was more money than he had ever seen in his life, all just sitting there in a figurative pile, and he had nothing that he could do with it. Enough money for a man to live in luxury for years, and he couldn't touch it because he knew that eventually, he was going to have to hand it all back with the shame of his failures exposed.

And to make matters worse, the money just kept on coming. He had already sold off a 50% stake in the fictitious business that was never going to go anywhere, and there were still more investors quietly pulling him aside at dinner parties with their chequebooks open. He had been so successful in generating excitement about his transportation revolution that everybody in Paris wanted a piece of it – and given that construction still hadn't started on his factory, he had no good reason to turn any of them down.

So the pressure went on mounting, and under such daunting stress, he began divesting himself of his other duties. The furniture business consisted of only him and a little rented warehouse, so he put it on a hiatus until he needed it again. He was able to hand off the day-to-day running of the garage to his more competent engineers to manage, while he only had to tackle the administrative duties himself. He was reluctant to let go of the reins of his biggest moneymakers, but he laughed at himself each time that feeling flared up. He was sitting on more money than he knew what to do with, why was he fretting over the few francs that his absence might have generated?

It is difficult to say at exactly what point his mind was made up, but at some point in late 1898, his plans changed. He recognised that while he did not have a product that he could sell for the millions that he meant to, he did have an idea that was worth just as much to potential investors. An idea that had already been so heavily invested into that the investment itself seemed like evidence that it was viable.

He remembered the first job as a clerk that he'd gotten coming out of the army. The smooth-talking man who had conned him out of his life savings in a bond. The man who had proven to him that the people who succeeded in life were not the ones who played by the rules and did the right thing, but the ones who were willing to seize every opportunity to grab what they wanted and damn the consequences.

Consequences. That had always been the concept that troubled the young Henri as he lay in bed at night. The consequences of doing the right thing were meant to be advancement and happiness, but experience had now proven to him that such things were rarely the payment for righteous behaviour. The consequences of doing bad things were supposed to be punishment. Yet when he had done everything right, been as obedient and diligent a young man as anyone could have ever asked, his repayment had been distrust and disdain. He had been taken advantage of by someone older, wiser, and more predatory, and been left with nothing, to claw his way out of a pit of debt. Meanwhile, the one who had robbed him had never faced any consequences at all. He had vanished with all of his money, never to return, and the police, those arbiters of justice who were meant to make things right when the balance was skewed, had done nothing to help him. They hadn't found the man, they hadn't retrieved his money, and they hadn't even checked back in to let him know that they'd found nothing. It had been as though he hadn't reported the crime at all.

It was as he sat there, hunched over his books, trying desperately to find some way out of this without his whole world crumbling down around him that an evil thought entered his mind and would not leave. What was to stop him from doing exactly the same as the man who'd robbed him? He had the money in his hand, what was to stop him from just running? His wife? She bored him. His kids? They'd be better off without him, he barely saw them as it was. With this money, he could go away, start over, and live a life of luxury and comfort. Drink champagne with a different woman every night. Lounge around in cafes. Do anything that he wanted, whenever he wanted. The only thing holding him back was him. The only thing stopping him from living a joyous life of hedonistic delights was his own choice not to do so.

So why did he persist in fighting so hard to keep a hold of this life that he didn't give a damn about? Because he wanted his father to be proud of him? His father was an idiot. He could barely understand a fraction of the things that Henri said to him. Why should he give up on everything that he desired to win the approval of a buffoon? It just didn't make sense.

If he did this, it would be an end to the promising future that he'd been trying to build for himself, for his family. He was not anonymous, he would not be able to take the money he'd accrued and go about his day. His name, his face, were well known in Paris and those investors that did come chasing after him when it became apparent that the factory was never going to be built would have no trouble tracking him down. Nor would the law, if the police could be prompted to pretend that they gave a damn. He would have to leave town, hide from sight, abandon everything that he'd ever known, lest they came after him and extract their money...or a pound of flesh.

These were all good reasons not to do it, yet somehow, he could not convince himself not to do it. Perhaps this was the temptation of the devil that they'd harped on about in church all these years. The temptation to take something instead of endlessly giving pieces of yourself away to ingrates who didn't appreciate it. Marie, the children, he loved them in his way, but it was in a very distant way. She had long ago lost her appeal, and the children were burdens through and through. As they grew older, perhaps they would become people that he might want to have something to do with, but as it stood, they were nothing to him but another expense of time and money that he just couldn't get the books to balance on.

Life without them would have been quieter, easier. Even if the whole city of Paris began to hate him, it would all be worthwhile just to be free of them. Them and his employees, and the cloying pseudo-friends that he'd ingratiated himself with so that he could build his businesses up from the ground. He couldn't even say that he hated them because that would have required some degree of passion. Rather, he was simply tired of them all. Their simpering smiles, their pointless stories, the boundless wealth at their beck and call, only because they had been born to the right parents.

Given their circumstances, Henri could have been ruling the world by now. And instead, here he was languishing in his office, night after night, trying desperately to make the impossible work so that he could make more money for those very same lucky bastards.

They didn't deserve it. They didn't deserve his effort, or his genius, or his kindness. They didn't deserve to get the money back that he had taken from them. That they had given away so freely in the hopes of exploiting him.

Henri was far too young to be having what we would now call a midlife crisis, but what he was experiencing was a crisis in faith. He had lost trust in the systems around him. He had lost trust that his efforts would be rewarded. He had lost trust in the institutions that he had once subscribed to and held dear. And without faith in a righteous world, there could be no fear of punishment.

The money was not enough. If he meant to elope with nothing but cash to his name, he wanted it to be more cash than he could ever use. Wealth to put Midas to shame. So much money that if he wanted, he could masquerade as one of those lucky bastards born into a fortune.

That should have been the point at which he stopped, backed down and calmed himself – returning to his normal life, and his normal problems – but that was not what Henri did. The realisation that there was not enough money to satisfy him did not turn him away from this new course – instead, he began doing what he did best. Making plans and designs.

He did not return home that night, spending the entirety of the time when he should have been in his bed scribbling out figures and calculations. Percentages and investments. Means of avoiding detection, and places where he could hide the wealth that he meant to claim for himself. He set out that morning, directly from his office, and began opening up bank accounts all over town. Using different names, and hastily produced false means of identification. The amount of money that he was flashing about was sufficient to make any banker salivate, and easily more than enough to make them set aside any doubts about the veracity of his paperwork.

Then, once his nest eggs were laid and preparations laid out, he moved on to the next phase of the plan. A good night's sleep, followed by a week full of appointments, working lunches and dinner dates.

He had sold off a 50% share of the Landru manufacturing business to investors. Within three days of actively courting more investors, the full 100% had been doled out. His company was no longer his own, it belonged entirely to his stakeholders and they could do what they pleased with it, and him. Then he sold some more, and some more, hiding investors that moved in different social circles from one another, falsifying papers and percentages. Making his original pitch about what an incredible machine the Landru was, and the ways that it was going to revolutionise city living, and selling to potential investors non-stop until finally, he decided that enough was enough. By that point, he had sold stocks and shares in his company equivalent to about 300% of its original estimated value.

Only then did he return home and pack some clothes for a "business trip", kiss his wife and children goodbye, and walk out the door, never intending to return for so long as he lived. At first, nothing changed. His employees had been made accustomed to working by themselves while the boss lurked in the back, handling the other facets of his business, so having him not show up at all made very little difference to them. They carried on with their working day and locked up when night fell. His family assumed that he would return soon from his trip, so showed no concern whatsoever over his absence. His investors had already been waiting so long without progress that they were becoming frustrated, but a day without contact from Henri was hardly a world-changing revelation for any of them.

Then another day passed, then another, a week, a month. Suddenly people noticed that he was gone, that he had vanished as though into thin air, and done so with such subtlety that people could not even pinpoint the last time that they saw him. Letters began to arrive, requesting his presence, questioning his whereabouts, and Marie had no clue how to answer. She herself had never lost faith that Henri would return, but she could find no trace of him.

The police were eventually involved as the various investors became aware of one another and the scale of the fraud that had been undertaken became public knowledge. Yet despite Henri's distinctive appearance and often flamboyant behaviour, they seemed entirely incapable of tracking him down. Just as he had turned his genius to the problems of machinery, so too had he directed his intellect to the game of cat and mouse that he knew was going to play out.

Those assets of his that the police could find were frozen, and over a long and arduous process, some portion of the money that he had taken was extracted from those accounts they could locate.

There was a great deal of debate at the time over whether Henri could have committed this scale of crime alone, and whether his wife could possibly have been unaware of his criminal intentions. Marie lived under constant suspicion and scrutiny, but through it all, she remained resolute. She had known nothing of what Henri was planning, nor had he provided her with any forwarding address. She had been as ardent in her own attempts to hunt him down as any one of the wealthy investors, as she had a far greater stake in this matter than any one of them. They had lost some small portion of their vast wealth, while she had lost the love of her life. The two were not comparable.

His garage had continued to run for as long as it could without leadership, but though Marie should technically have inherited ownership in Henri's absence, it was considered an asset of his and stripped down for anything of worth by those he owed money. All his staff lost their jobs. His inventions and any notes left behind in the workshop were seized and handed around amongst the technically minded in the hopes that there might have at least been something patentable that could return some portion of a profit, but while Henri had come up with a great many ideas, they were not novel in any way. If he had continued with his higher education, he most likely would have encountered precisely the things that he himself had invented to solve problems that had already been solved long ago. Even the Landru motorbike prototype was seized, and it was then that the discovery was made that it was not the technological advance that Henri had promised, but a completely normal motorbike, albeit one that had been constructed through a roundabout process utilizing an amalgamation of existing and newly fabricated parts assembled in a mash-up much like a machine version of Frankenstein's monster. The only thing distinctive about the Landru was its aesthetics, and those were not considered to be in its favour. A genius in his field, Henri may have been, but a designer he was not.

And still, the hunt went on, police and private investigators tripping over one another as they tried to find Herni Landru and make him face justice for what he had done. Primarily private investigators, given that the police had rapidly arrived at the same conclusion as Henri himself about his investors; that it wouldn't do people this rich any harm to lose a little bit of money.

The Landru family that he had left behind had lost all of their savings once more, with the various lawsuits against Henri frittering it away to nothing. Destitute, Marie and the children survived only through the kindness of their family and community. Primarily the former, as the community had mostly turned on her when she was suspected of aiding and abetting her criminal husband.

On the Ile Saint-Louis, the list of Deacons of the church was silently edited to remove Henri Landru's name. As though the man no longer existed at all. If he had died, his erasure would not have been so complete, because at least his memory would still have been acknowledged, but among those people that he had spent his life serving and helping, he was treated now as an "un-person". Someone shunned, someone who you could not even acknowledge as existing without drawing the ire of the community. His parents and siblings were still allowed to attend services and take mass, provided they kept his name out of their mouths, but his wife and children were a different matter. They were never officially excommunicated, but it was made abundantly clear that they were no longer welcome to worship on the Ile Saint-Louis. There were a thousand other churches in Paris where they might take communion and worship, where knowledge of her criminal husband had not yet spread, but he had brought shame upon everyone that attended the church where he had served as Deacon. A shame of association that would only be worsened if they continued to offer succour and shelter to the woman who most believed to be his willing accomplice.

Destitute and abandoned, Marie and her children sank into poverty and misery, while somewhere out there, she knew that Henri was still alive and well, enjoying the good life as a result of all the money that he had embezzled.

After Ever After

For his first year in exile, Henri laid low in the city of Le Havre on France's northern coast. It was a port town, the second largest in all of France, and the constant movement of new residents and those drifting through provided an ideal smoke screen for a man on the run.

He had money now, enough that if he were careful he would never have to work again, but Henri was not inclined to be careful. He had already proven to himself just how easy money was to come by when you were smarter than everyone else, so why should he worry about splurging and enjoying himself? If he ran out of cash, all he'd need to do was make some more with another clever ploy.

Access to his bank accounts was more limited than he would have liked, so a great deal of the money that he had put away for rainy days was inaccessible. He could never be certain which of his false identities the police were aware of, so there was an element of risk every time that he tapped into a new identity's accounts. For this reason, he worked his way very carefully through them while trying to avoid drawing attention to himself.

Having ready money made it much easier for him to pursue women, which seemed to be his primary activity now that he was no longer sharing lodgings with his wife. Almost every night he could be seen dining out with a different woman on his arm. Whatever else may have changed throughout his life, his lust for the fairer sex had never declined, and neither had his enviable ability to talk glibly with them to the point that almost any lie became believable.

More often than not, he would stick to the same simple ruse, simply because it was easier to remember. He was a wealthy widower, a business owner, seeking companionship and perhaps more. The promise of the potential for marriage in their future to a man who could ably provide for them was more than enough for the vast majority of the women that he pursued, but for those who believed that they deserved more, he always had another yarn to spin. About the future projects he meant to pursue, the car manufactory that he intended to build once he had raised enough money from investors, the various investments that he had already made which were returning hefty dividends and that he expected to make him millions in the coming years, the line of mechanical toys for children that he had in development.

For the women who had no interest in the finer things in life, there was Henri himself, as romantic and charming a man as any one of them might ever hope to meet. Even women who sought out their partners solely on the basis of physical appeal, an area that Henri would readily admit that he could never compete in, there was a degree of charisma that belied his plain and eccentric appearance – an intensity to him that seemed to be greater than the sum of his parts.

In truth, all of the lying and romancing that he was undertaking in Le Havre was hardly new to him. Much as his wife would have claimed otherwise, he had always had an eye for women, and as blinded as Marie might have been, even she could recognize from an early age that he was what was referred to at the time as a "skirt chaser." No small part of her misery in his absence came from the belief that he had likely just absconded with some pretty young thing. As though her inability to hold his attention as she grew older and lost her girlish looks were some sort of flaw in her character, rather than a gaping hole in his.

He had been unfaithful to her many times throughout their relationship, both while he was off in the army and after he had returned home, though at least in Paris he had the good grace to be subtle about it. Even so, for all that the city was huge, word still got around, and it got back to her all too quickly.

There was a great deal of denial in Marie, denial that her husband was truly a criminal, denial that he had abandoned her and her children to destitution, denial of his fundamentally weak character. Of course, she had denied that he was being unfaithful to her.

She would defend him, even when the police came around asking after him again and again. This was all just a misunderstanding, he must have been stranded abroad during his business trip, there was no way that he would have just left her here with all those children to feed. He was, in her words, a "model husband." Something that even his closest friends and family beyond her simply could not attest to. Even if they did still hold out hope that he would resurface and make all of this right.

The funny thing was, she was closer to the truth than she knew.

Henri enjoyed his time on the coast, but before the year was up he was thoroughly bored and wondering if he might be able to sneak back to Paris unnoticed and get back to the quality of life that he was more accustomed to. It wasn't that the people in Le Havre were boring as such, it was just that they were in constant flux – he felt like there was nobody who actually lived there – they were all just passing through, and when a man on the run from the law had stayed in one place longer than all of his neighbours, it suggested that something was off. He did not dare return to Paris immediately, however, he needed someone to scout things out for him and let him know if it was safe.

Accordingly, he sent a letter to his wife full of apologies and lies about where he had been and where he was now. He included in his letter detailed instructions on how she could gain access to one of the bank accounts that he had been too nervous to touch, and which contained so little by comparison to his other nest eggs that he hadn't really fussed about not being able to get it.

Even if the witless woman reported back that everything was safe, that bank account would serve as a nice test to see how the city responded to some of his assets coming back to life. If the police showed up at her door the day after she tried to get at the money, he would know that they were still monitoring for his return and he would book passage to somewhere further afield before his idiot wife gave away his location somehow. If she got the money without a problem, then perhaps the storm had passed and he would no longer need to hide out.

It took considerably longer than he would have liked to finally receive an answer from her, and to his delight he discovered that Marie was as gullible as ever, believing every word that he said without question and following his instructions to the letter. It seemed that she was able to access the account without issue and that the private investigators that had once buzzed around their home like flies around rotten meat had now departed for more promising carrion. If he wanted, he could come home.

It took him months to make up his mind. Returning home may have had its appeal, including the creature comforts that he was accustomed to, and the lifestyle which he was craving, but there were an abundance of downsides too. Even beyond the need to pay out for the maintenance of Marie and the other parasites, there would be danger involved, problems that he really didn't feel any abiding need to confront. He would be instantly recognisable to anyone that he had defrauded, so it would be necessary to remain on high alert and avoid those circles in which people of that sort moved unless he could be certain that they would not be about. Lying to all of his old friends would be no great effort, he had barely told them the truth even when he had nothing to hide, the only real difficulty would be in tricking people into falling for the same scam all over again.

Yet fall for it they did. Almost as soon as he had returned to Paris and moved back into the family home, Henri started fishing for new investors for his latest projects. A train line running out into the suburbs from the centre of town, the sort of civic development that might be named after whichever backer invested the most money, securing their legacy throughout history. A factory for cars. The long-discussed automated children's toy. Every idea he had ever concocted in his life was transformed into something real and plausible by his words, with technical details that would have entirely escaped someone without his background and intellect. Enough to convince even the dubious that they were dealing with an expert on the subject. One by one, the lines that he had dropped into the water began to get bites. Franc by franc, his depleted reserves of ready money became refilled, and he was able to begin putting on a show of wealth and success once more. The more successful he seemed, the more easily his marks were duped, and the more of them that were duped, the more money he had to look successful.

In truth, being on the run from the law was a blessing in disguise for Henri, because it allowed him to entirely sidestep many of the problems that he had anticipated. He did not have to see his family, knowing how they would damn him and curse his name for his wicked ways; because if he were to see them then it would implicate them in his crimes. He did not have to linger around the house with his insipid wife and boring children, not when he was on the run and the police might show up on their doorstep at any moment. He had to keep on the move, or so he told Marie, so as to prevent any of the people who felt like he'd cheated them in a deal from finding him and exacting their revenge. His life was in danger, according to him, endangered by the very people that he had sought to help, who had failed to understand his genius and demanded money back from him that he hadn't yet had time to make. They were greedy men, these investors, seeking to fleece him out of every penny that he had rather than giving him the time to bring his bright ideas for the future to fruition. He actually restarted his untouched used furniture business during this time, despite the incongruity of it. Not because he believed that he could make a fortune buying and selling old chairs, but because of the valuable contacts that it afforded him. In particular, he began paying close attention to letters from older women, widows and the like, who had fallen on hard times and needed help getting their finances back in order. For them, he was like a heaven-sent angel, not only offering them extraordinary prices on pieces of furniture worth less than the materials they'd been crafted from but also sitting down with them to go through their accounts and books to help them understand where their dead husbands' wealth had been buried. And those that he helped to excavate such things were always so grateful to him that when he suggested that it might be worth investing some portion of their good fortune to provide them with dividends to live off in the future, they were more than happy to trust him with it entirely.

At first, he lived comfortably off his takings from these unfortunate women, vanishing when the time came that they started to ask too many questions. Then he simply scaled up his business model, securing the money and vanishing instantly, ignoring any follow-up he may have received from them under a plethora of false identities. As it turned out, he did not need a good reputation to carry him in the business of secondhand furniture, all he needed was to show up and be charismatic – and nine times out of ten the battle was already won.

The spoils of these victories ranged from pathetic little dribbles of cash to lifelong savings that he could make off with, and because of the way that families were structured in the time period, the women were often none the wiser either way. There were as many grand dames who had been living in the lap of luxury with the wolf at the door as there were grey-faced unfortunates living like church mice who had a small fortune stowed away in savings that their dead husbands had refused to touch for some reason or another. The world of finances had deliberately barred the doors against women to keep them from gaining too much independence, and the net result was that they were supremely vulnerable to a man like Henri who could not only parse all of the information but manipulate it to give them whatever impression he desired.

There were of course a few women out there that he encountered, fool enough to be taken in by his rhetoric but wise enough to understand what they had and what he had taken. They were the ones to file police reports about the defrauding that had become Henri's bread and butter. Police reports that detailed a spate of white-collar crimes that half the officers hunting the perpetrator couldn't even understand properly, which had been committed by a wide variety of different characters. Names that Henri had pulled out of his hat on the way to the appointment rather than one of his longstanding false identities. He never meant to see these women again after that first day, so why bother to keep his stories straight?

Yet it was not one of his great schemes that saw him caught in the end, not the railway line, the car factory, the automatic toy, or any of the grandiose promises that he'd made to the wealthy of the city, but one of the cheques that he had tricked an elderly widow out of.

She had realised more quickly than most that he had broken trust with her. She managed to recall a horror story passed along to her through the grapevine about a con artist tricking women out of their pensions before he had already been to the bank and absconded with the money. She asked a neighbour to run to the bank with a note about the situation, giving them warning that she did not consent to the man taking money from her account in her absence.

Henri strode into the bank as bold as day without even a hint of hesitation. And why would he have hesitated when he had gotten away with the same thing a dozen times or more? There were a hundred older women in the city of Paris now bereft of the nest egg that their husbands had left behind for them, and not one of them had had the wherewithal to intervene before now. All experience had taught Henri that he could do anything he wanted without consequences, so what need was there for worries?

He smiled at the cashier with all his usual charm and chatted away with her, running through his usual script of pleasant small talk as he waited for her to process the cheque and hand him his cash, so both of them seemed equally surprised when it turned out that she couldn't. He frowned then, for a moment, a tiny crack in his veneer of personability, but he wiped it away swiftly, an incompetent cashier was hardly the end of the world, he could always go to another branch later and sort things out. It was a slight nuisance in his day, but not anything truly important.

So when he asked for the cheque back so he could go sort things out later, imagine his surprise when the cashier refused. She had to hold the cheque, she had her orders from the manager that she couldn't return it. He'd have to go back to whoever issued the cheque, sort out the situation, and return with a fresh one if he was going to get a single franc.

This was more than a nuisance. He couldn't even remember what story he'd spun to the particular widow in question, nor did he have any plans of going back into a situation where he was already being treated as a suspect. For all he knew the police or her family might have already been gathered there to pick him up or beat him down. There was too much risk involved in a second visit, and he had no intention of putting himself at risk.

So, he demanded the cheque back. He insisted that it be returned to him, he was not going to trouble the poor woman who had written it again over some banking error. He refused. Despite this sudden outburst of irritation from the most amiable of customers setting the clerk on their back foot, still she stuck to her guns. If she let Henri leave here with the cheque, she would be in dereliction of her duty as a banker.

The argument went back and forth in furious whispers for several minutes, and all the while that Henri was delayed, the manager of the bank was off down the street to the nearest constabulary, fetching help to apprehend a fraudster in the act.

Too late, Henri seemed to realise the danger that he was in, storming out of the bank, claiming that he would never do business there again. But losing a great deal of the breath that he would have used yelling as he broke into a brisk jog through the bank's lobby. Out in the street, his head jerked around, seeking any sign of the police, but it seemed that he had made it unscathed this time.

He took off at a full-on run across the street, heading away from the bank at top speed, panting and gasping from the unexpected exercise with every step. He was not accustomed to this level of physical activity, he considered himself to be above it. Manual labour and scurrying around, those were jobs for lesser minds, like his father.

He made it a good distance before tripping over a loose cobblestone and twisting his ankle. At once the kindly people of Paris came rushing to his aid, a crowd completely surrounding him, helping him back to his feet, carrying him as much as assisting him in walking to a seat outside a nearby café and then fussing over him. Old women chastising him for being in such a hurry that he hurt himself. A doctor surfacing out of the crowd and insisting upon looking at his ankle. One of the waitstaff rushing out with ice bundled in a rag. He was pinned in place by their kindness, and of course, the crowd drew the attention of the bank manager and police as they came in their own rush down the street and immediately spotted him.

The bank manager identified him on the spot, and before he had even had the opportunity to open his mouth and explain himself, one of the officers recognised him as Henri Landru, the famous motorcycle inventor and fraudster. The cuffs were on him before the ice on his ankle had even melted, and the crowd that had so overwhelmed him with kindness now turned angry, realising that they had given their empathy to a criminal. He had to be hauled off to the station dangling like a limp sack between two of the police officers before things turned ugly.

So it was that for the first time in his life, Henri faced the consequences of his actions. The greater frauds that he had perpetuated were legally complex and difficult to unpick, but the simple defrauding of the poor old widow was easy for a judge and the court to understand. Given the morally abhorrent nature of the crime, preying upon the most vulnerable in society, when summary judgement was handed down it came with the heaviest punishment possible for the judge to assign. Two years imprisonment in Fresnes Jail, south of Paris.

Still, he was not without tricks up his sleeve to try and get out of the situation. While he was still remanded to Santé Prison awaiting transfer, he made the case for his own insanity. He made a noose out of his bedsheets, slipping them around his neck and then stepping off the bedframe when he heard one of the guards opening his cell door.

To the custodial officers, it was obvious that this was a fake suicide attempt, but it was still reported, and Henri still had to be passed into the hands of the doctors before he could be shipped off to serve his sentence.

One of Paris' premier doctors of psychiatry was called in to study Henri and judge whether he was mentally competent or had slipped over the precipice into madness that would require him to receive treatment rather than punishment by the system.

Dr Charles Vallon examined Henri, and they spent over a week in sessions together. As it was obviously in Henri's best interests to be found insane, he made sure to share every dark thought that had ever crossed his mind with the psychiatrist, reframing every minor inconvenience that he had suffered into catastrophic traumas and constructing a narrative of a descent into criminality born of madness after his worldview was shattered by his own defrauding by a fake employer making off with his savings all of those years ago.

It was a difficult case for Dr Vallon, for obvious reasons. It was not often that he was called upon to study so intelligent a subject, who was so obviously engaging in subterfuge, carefully picking every word to get the desired result. After many sessions, he would leave unsure if a single word that Henri had spoken was entirely true, and he had to rely upon seeking out evidence from the police records to verify any one of Henri's tales.

Eventually, he concluded that while Henri Landru was "on the frontiers of madness" he had not yet fully crossed over, and as such could be considered to be fully responsible for his own actions and suffer the consequences as such. However, he was so convinced of Landru's burgeoning sickness that he paid a visit to his wife Marie to detail all that he had learned and to ask that she see to it that Henri was placed into care at the very moment he showed any further signs of instability.

Now, in Marie's mind, her beloved husband had an excuse. He had not abandoned her and their children, he had been in the throes of a terrible madness. He was no longer a villain to be loathed, but a victim of his own awful circumstances. The doctor requests that she seek help for him at the first sign of a return to criminality after his custodial sentence completely sealed the deal for her. She would stand by her poor sick husband until his dying day.

Finally, Henri was shipped off to serve his time in Fresnes, far enough from Paris that it would not be possible for Marie to visit him with any sort of regularity. He would be serving hard labour there – something that he was completely unsuited to, and complained about bitterly, claiming that such a punishment was essentially a death sentence for so physically delicate a man. He wrote letters complaining of the inhumanity of his treatment, even entreating Dr Vallon to intercede on his behalf, explaining that such treatment was liable to exacerbate his mental problems and drive him to more violent crime after his release. If they truly meant to rehabilitate him, then surely torture was not the answer. Not to mention that if he were given a more mentally stimulating task, he was certain that he could be of more benefit to society. Why not have him manage the prison's finances, or tackle administrative duties? He would even accept his old job as a quartermaster, although he understood that the pay would be greatly reduced due to the shift in circumstances. In short, he spent every day in prison complaining as though he were a disgruntled tourist at an all-inclusive resort that was failing to live up to his expectations.

In truth, the prison was not much of a deterrent to Henri. He was not considered to be a particularly dangerous criminal, so he was given a lot of leeway, and his ever-present charisma allowed him to navigate, with a minimum of risk, the cliques and social situations that might have tripped others. The fact that he always had more money than he knew how to spend definitely helped him to make friends too. Admittedly, he was not living in the lap of luxury as he liked to when he was in command of his own destiny, dining at the finest restaurants with the most beautiful of women, but the poor quality of things in prison reminded him of his childhood. Each day's slop in the cafeteria, a new reminiscence about his mother's cooking. Every night returning to the stale sweat smell of his cell, a reminder of his father staggering home from work, too sore to even move.

For all of his complaining, there was nothing that Henri was experiencing in prison that was new to him, and certainly, nothing that might have done him any harm, given that he'd already survived it.

Yet as comfortable as Henri may have been in his new home, the same cannot be said for those that were closest to him.

While Marie had her mind made up about Henri being a tragic figure suffering from mental illness, that was not the impression that the rest of Paris had of the man. They considered him to be the very worst sort of criminal reprobate, robbing the poor and the bereaved to line his own pockets. More and more civil suits were filed against him as his various investors from across the years attempted to recoup their losses, and while Marie had nothing at all, and no access to Henri's many hidden accounts, it was still her that they pursued. She was dragged through the courts time and time again to account for her husband's actions, and while she always claimed ignorance, there was no shortage of people ready to doubt her. She had dealt with some degree of this sort of shaming already and was inured to it, but the rest of Henri's family were not so thick-skinned.

His father was overcome by shame when he learned that his son had been convicted of the crimes which he had been accused of. As a result of his son's actions, his own reputation as an upstanding citizen was now being called into question. It was true that he lacked the intellectual capacity that defined his son.

He wasn't simple-minded, as such, but he had a simple and direct way of approaching problems that Henri looked upon with contempt. If he made a mistake, he would admit to it, and do what he could to make it right. If he had done something wrong, he would apologise and promise to never do it again. But this new guilt that he felt, for raising a son who could commit such monstrous acts as defrauding widows of their pensions, he didn't have a simple solution to that. He tried to make his apologies to the community at large, but they were rebuffed. He tried to make contrition at church, but the priests requested that he start worshipping elsewhere in the city where his face and name were not so well known. Everywhere that he went, he had been made a pariah. All the good and kind folk of Paris wanted nothing to do with him.

So once again, he took the direct approach to the problem of his life as a respected member of the community being over. Just as his son had fashioned a noose in his jail cell to try and find an escape from his current situation, so too did his father. He used a good length of rope instead of twisted bedsheets, and he tied the knot tight so that there was no chance of it slipping loose. Then when he was certain that he'd have privacy in the home for a few hours, he slung the rope over the tree, pulled his amended last will and testament out of the family chest, and hung himself.

While Henri was spending his first day in the Fresnes Jail, complaining to all and sundry about his mattress being too firm and the work expected of him too much, his father was swinging from side to side from the bough of a tree in the Bois de Boulogne.

Rather than live with the shame of having a son like Henri, his father took his own life, leaving his wife and children to fend for themselves. There was a good portion of money set aside for them, to keep them all in some degree of comfort until the kids were making enough to help support their mother, but to Henri, not a single penny was to be given. Instead, his portion of the inheritance was to be paid to Marie and her children, and only to Marie and her children. Some wondered if that was why he had killed himself when he had, to ensure that Henri was out of the picture and couldn't lay hands on it.

Marie was torn. On the one hand, the money would make it so that she didn't have to work twelve-hour days in the laundry to keep a roof over her head, but on the other, it was an inheritance from Henri's father. To take it for herself just because they weren't seeing eye to eye at the moment of his death, that seemed treacherous somehow. As though she was one of those inheritance chasers marrying old men for what they'd leave behind. She tried to eliminate the problem and divest herself of guilt by turning the money over to Henri's mother. She was an old woman before her time after a lifetime of exhausting labour, unable to work for herself, she was reliant upon the charity of the church and the kindness of her children to keep herself fed. If there was anyone in the world who deserved the money that her husband had squirrelled away it was her. Yet she refused it outright.

That money had been put aside for Marie and the children. It had been put aside for them from the very moment that Henri had first disappeared, some of it already hidden under the mattress on the day that they married. However slow of mind his father may have been, it seemed that he had understood his son perfectly well. He had understood from the beginning that the boy would not be faithful, that he would not do the right thing and stand by his family, he had known the moral failings of Henri Landru before everyone else, but he had still waited and tried to give him the chance to do better. He had spent Henri's whole life hoping that he'd redeem himself from the darkest parts of his character.

He was consigned to a potter's field outside of Paris, both because the destitution of his family required the state to pay for his disposal, and because as a suicide he had committed a sin so grievous he could not be consigned to the consecrated soil of a Catholic churchyard, nor receive a Catholic ceremony of burial. By the logic that he followed, he had damned himself. For the love of his son, and sorrow over how low he had fallen, Henri's father had consigned his own soul to hell. For a soft-spoken man disinclined to dramatic gestures, it certainly should have made his point clear.

In prison, news of his father's death by his own hand reached Henri. The shocking and sad news was passed down through official channels rather than conveyed to him by a visiting family member as would have been proper. He took it with surprising grace. The guards had half expected some sort of outburst, as would have been understandable, but instead there was an almost eerie silence.

He went back to his life in prison as if he'd received no news, going through the usual motions, making his usual regular complaints. A few guards thought that he was trying to play off their sympathy for the loss of his father to get better treatment, but it did not take any of them long to realise that he was just behaving as he always did. As though nothing had changed.

In truth, Henri was extremely ambivalent about his father's death. He had convinced himself that it wouldn't matter to him when the old man died because he had already mentally severed all connections between them when he decided to pursue his shameful career in crime. He had meticulously gone through every connection in his mind between the imposing figure of his father and his nascent sense of morality and cauterised each one. His father had represented his childhood, his old life, when he believed in the simple lies that children were told. Lies like decency and justice. He had severed all ties to the man in the same moment that he had broken away from such basic ideas of morality.

Yet now, he could feel the weight of his father's death in his gut. Despite his superior intellect, despite all of the distance that he had set between them, despite everything that he had done in his life, he had never been able to bring himself to hate his father. It would have been like hating a doe-eyed puppy. The man was gentle and kind to a fault, the antithesis of everything that Henri had been striving to make himself into. And so long as the man lived, Henri had still felt his eyes upon him, judging him for his actions. He might not have believed in any heavenly father looking down at him and commanding him to be righteous, but he could quite perfectly picture what his father's pained and sorrowful expression would have looked like every time that he did something he knew the old man would have thought of as wrong.

All of his life, the man had just watched Henri making mistakes. He was strong enough to stop anyone from doing anything that he didn't want them doing, but he had always just sat back with that same sorrowful expression, letting his children make their own decisions and learning from them instead of snatching away the opportunity. And it had worked so well with the others, they had learned their lessons, they had grown to be moral and upstanding members of the community. They had followed in their father's footsteps to become sheep, herded along by the powerful and the wealthy, always believing that tomorrow would be better despite all evidence to the contrary, so long as they just kept on following the rules. Henri was the only one who had seen through it, the only one who had broken free of society's expectations of him, and he was repaid like this, jail time.

The truth of the matter was that regardless of whether he had successfully disassociated his father as a holy arbiter of justice from himself or not, he had still been held back in some way by the lingering fear of disappointing the man. They had never seen eye to eye, never even gotten along really, but all the same, he was Henri's father and he felt beholden to him, to at least some degree.

Now that the connection was severed in truth as well as in Henri's imagination, it was impossible to predict what he would be capable of.

Escalation

Henri was released from prison in autumn of 1912. Having been made temporarily destitute by the seizure of all his assets when he was arrested, and labouring under the somewhat correct idea that the police would no longer be pursuing him, given the length of time that they'd had him at their mercy and brought no more charges, he returned home to his family.

Marie was over the moon. Her husband had finally returned to her after all this time. He was back in her life, in her children's lives, all previous sins expunged, and ready to start anew. She would keep a close watch on him, as the doctor had instructed. Keep an eye out for any hint that his mental illness was going to snatch him from her again. She stood ready to condemn him to an asylum if she truly feared for his safety. But none of these things seemed to be necessary.

He was a changed man. All of the philandering, the lying, it was all in the past, and now he wanted nothing more than to get his life back in order and live as he was meant to.

For work, he took on small jobs with local garages, nobody would trust him with much more than grunt work, but his understanding of machines still shone through, and eventually, he was drawn into a sort of consulting arrangement with many of them. He would visit by night when the customers were not around to see him and ruin the company's reputation, and provide the garages with the solutions that they themselves could not reach. He passed every penny that he made on to Marie but lamented that he had so little capital to work with. If he had just a little money, he could have kick-started his furniture business again and really begun building a future for them.

This was her first temptation, and she did not succumb. It was still too soon; the wounds of his past betrayals were still too raw. She did not offer him the money that his father had left. But neither did she feel entitled to every penny that he made working his odd jobs. So she gave him leave to spend what he needed of the family's money to get things going again. The family's money in this case being extremely little, in truth. What she earned as a washerwoman and what he had managed to scrape together over the past few months were mere pennies compared to what he had once walked around with in his money clip but however meagre the amount, it was enough for him to start buying new stock.

His charisma had always served him well when it came to purchasing new stock, and the vast majority of the dealers whom he had provided furniture for in the past were completely unaware of his criminal dealings or custodial sentence. He slipped back into the old patterns of behaviour so smoothly that Marie feared that soon she'd be hearing tales of his latest affair. But somehow, he managed to keep his nose clean. He was not defrauding anyone unless you counted the odd piece of furniture that he bought for less than it was worth.

He had money now. Enough that he could abscond any time he pleased. Marie was braced for it. Had been braced for it from the moment that she gave him free rein over his own finances once more, but even now that there was paper money in his pocket, he was showing no interest in heading out into the world and seeking his freedom. In fact, now that he was turning a profit, Marie was delighted to discover that piece by piece, the old hand-me-down furniture in their home was being replaced with high-quality furnishings. The walls were freshly painted. The bills paid off well ahead of time. There was enough money in their shared account that she no longer had to count her pennies each time that she wanted to buy some milk.

All the years of toil and suffering seemed to be at an end. Just like every other victim that Henri had conned through the years, she was convinced that now, finally her life was going to turn around, she was going to be comfortable and happy.

When she came home to find him sitting with their family account books laid out before him on the kitchen table and an expression of distress, she was of course concerned. But he took care to alleviate her fears. They were fine, they had everything that they needed, and they were well provided for. He had simply wished to do more, he wanted to make things up to her, to give her the kind of life that she deserved, and he couldn't. She tried to convince him that she was satisfied, that she did not need the wealth that his genius had promised in their youth, but this only seemed to upset him more. He felt a strong sense of guilt about his family giving her everything he had promised and to make matters worse, he had found exactly the opportunity to do so. One of the garages that he consulted for was up for sale, a flourishing business that he could take over tomorrow if he just had the money. It would mean no more travelling; he would be coming home every night at the same time to share his dinner and evenings with her. All of the little things that she had been missing throughout their whole marriage, all the little implied promises that he had never kept. If only he had, say, 12,000 francs to make the initial investment.

He did not have that money. No matter how he tried to balance the books. Even if he sold off everything he owned, he would not have enough. And the offer was time sensitive, it would only take weeks before one of the garage's competitors came sniffing around and snatched the place up. It was one of the most profitable businesses in the city, of course, it wasn't going to stay on the market for more than a few days!

He did not have 12,000 francs, but Marie did. It was almost exactly what she had been left by Henri's father when the man killed himself. A coincidence that did not entirely escape her attention. She loved Henri, she believed in Henri, but she was not entirely blind to the man's faults. If he had come to her in the first week out of prison with all the play-acting of distress, then she would have immediately clocked it as a con, but this Henri... he was different. He had changed. He had learned, and grown, and he wanted to do better for her and their whole family.

In short, she had been tricked just as easily as all the other women he had taken in over the years. She went to the bank, handed over the only savings that she had in the world to

Henri and with a smile on his face he set off to buy them the future that they wanted.

He did not return.

It is about this time that it becomes apparent that Henri's constant scheming and plotting was no longer an attempt to acquire wealth, so much as it was his baseline level of operation. Even though he was flush with his stolen inheritance and had no financial needs, he was on the grind all the same, posting advertisements, posing as a wealthy widower, setting up the groundwork for a new investment fraud – this time involving a fictitious massive automobile factory just outside of the city of Paris – and generally behaving as though he were in one of his previously established cycles of poverty and excess on the opposite side of the coin from where he actually was.

At some point, the thrill of his victories overtook financial gain as his motivation. And this would become increasingly apparent as many of the women that he seduced for their fortunes in the coming months had very little to give him. It was as though the act of robbing them, of tricking them out of their belongings and achieving some sort of financial domination over them was the whole goal of the exercise. He had a slew of lovers that he eventually defrauded, but it was for such small sums that they didn't even bother to file reports with the police. Many of them were simply confused by his bizarre choices, especially given that he clearly had no shortage of his own money to work with.

Before 1914 he had perpetrated only two notably successful cons, both defrauding widows of their inheritance. One of these was in Paris, the other in the northern town of Lille, on the border of Belgium. Madame Izore was the latter, left destitute after Henri convinced her that they would be wed, and she turned over her full fortune of 15,000 francs as a dowry. By the time the matter was being brought to court, Henri had already been imprisoned in Paris for the other successful fraud.

He was due to serve multiple years for the repeated acts of fraud that he had committed against the people of Paris, probably taking him out of circulation for the foreseeable future and rendering all his scheming and planning pointless. But there were other factors at play in the world that would shape his future now.

The Great War had just broken out. The German War Machine was in motion. Surrounded on both sides by enemies, the Kaiser devised an aggressive and seemingly ingenious strategy to turn an inevitable, crushing defeat into two difficult battles on opposing fronts. Mobility and rapid deployment, the hallmarks of modern warfare, were on the German side, while France had not fought a serious land war in decades, and Russia, on the other side, was notoriously slow to bring their forces to bear. The German plan was simple, they had to defeat France before the Russians could join the war, then swivel their full force to the eastern front to face the more powerful aggressor once the foe was defeated.

The Alsace Line stood in their way, the whole connecting border between Germany and France was lined with fortified emplacements with heavy artillery at the ready, an impenetrable wall. Bringing all of their forces to bear, it was possible that eventually, Germany might have been able to punch through, but by then, the delay would have proven lethal, and Russian troops would be nipping at their heels.

France fully expected to hold that line for as long as it took with their existing army. They had no fear of invasion on that front and total faith in their defences. But the Kaiser was nothing if not resourceful. He was already gambling heavily in his stratagems, and so he added one final roll of the dice.

Belgium was a neutral party in the war, a small place with little in the way of armed forces. Their only real defence against German aggression was the fact that they had a treaty with Great Britain that would have drawn the United Kingdom into a war with any force that violated their territory. Once more the Kaiser was gambling that he could win his war before his enemies had a chance to deploy their troops – if he used the element of surprise. Swinging a vast force north to the sea, the Germans marched through Belgium, obliterating the local defenders and arriving on French soil within spitting distance of Lille, drawing Britain into the war, but winning them the first true victory of the whole engagement.

For obvious reasons, the arrival of a massive modern army on French soil sent the leadership in Paris into something of a panic. They scrabbled to fill their ranks as swiftly as possible, calling on all army veterans to return to their posts, so that this new threat to French sovereignty might be turned back before the German forces could punch through into the heart of France.

As a part of this desperate struggle for bodies to fill uniforms, a law was passed that allowed for the pardoning and release of any criminal in French prisons who had previously served in the army, so that they might do their patriotic duty and return to the front lines.

Under this law, even though he was still awaiting trial for his crimes in Lille, Henri found himself back on the streets of

Paris with a slip of paper directing him to the nearest recruitment office so he could be fitted for a uniform and get back out there to defend his homeland.

Henri had no interest in defending his homeland. He did not give a damn about France any more than he gave a damn about anything else. He had done well in the army – not out of some patriotic fervour, but because it made his life easier for him when he did well. He had heard tales of what modern warfare looked like from those unfortunate enough to have friends out on the front lines. The nightmarish bombardment of artillery. The horrors of trench warfare, of poisonous gas being released from barrels on the battlefield, seeping across, blinding men and burning out lungs. He had no intention of putting himself in harm's way, and he certainly didn't intend to do it for the good of the nation of France which had so far repaid his genius by repeatedly imprisoning him and depriving him of his ill-gotten gains. Given the opportunity to be free, Henri took it, vanishing into the Parisian underworld before his absence could even be noted.

It was about this time that his grandest ever con came to fruition. He had planted the seeds before his imprisonment, and now it was time to reap the harvest. Despite all of the chaos raking France, cars were still going to be needed. In fact, grand factories capable of manufacturing mechanical parts were about to become extremely valuable, and now would be the ideal time to invest in them, even if automobiles in general held no appeal. It was practically the patriotic duty of every rich idiot to throw their money into the infrastructure that would allow France to drive back the Germans and ensure peace, freedom, fraternity, equality, and all of that other good stuff.

In a matter of weeks, he appeared in the lives of the Parisian wealthy that he had not already bilked and laid out his plans. Within days he had signed up twelve investors for a grand total of 35,600 Francs, guaranteeing them rapid returns and the warm feeling that could only come from helping their great nation with its war efforts.

But the world was not so innocent and gullible as it had been when Henri began his criminal career. Nor was he half so credible now. Those wealthy men who had invested some portion of their fortune into his factory soon became concerned over the lack of progress, made inquiries about Henri, and learned the truth of his duplicitous nature. To lose a little money and a little face to a trickster was one thing, but Henri had played off of their patriotism, and for that, it was felt he should be punished to the fullest extent of the law. All twelve of his investors filed complaints with the police, simultaneously, in late March of 1914, delivering along with their complaint a full litany of all Henri's previous crimes that they had uncovered; the evidence pertaining to said crimes, the names and addresses for all of the previous complainants, and essentially everything that would be required to make any sort of case against Henri Landru stick. The wealthy of Paris may have been a lackadaisical lot as a general rule, but when they felt that a wrong had been done to them, there was no denying their efficiency or the efficiency of the many private investigators that had been hired through the years as a result of their fairly correct assumption that the police of Paris would be too incompetent to pull together a case against Henri on their own.

At the beginning of April, the police raided Landru's home, much to the amusement of his estranged wife, who asked that they also retrieve the money he'd stolen from her if they had the opportunity. From there, their hunt for him led them in circles for some time until eventually, they came upon the apartment where he liked to entertain lady guests in Paris. It had been stripped bare of its fine furnishings several weeks before, and they had been sold off to finance Landru's rapid departure from the city. Whether he had been tipped off by some informant within the police department about his impending arrest, or he had simply connected the dots himself, it mattered little. Henri was on the run again.

Unwilling to wait for justice to be served given the period of global instability that was currently underway, the offended parties pressured the French legal system into action, and a trial was conducted in Landru's absence. Henri was convicted of the massive fraud that he had undertaken and sentenced to four years of hard labour. Indeed, when all of his other crimes were taken into account, an additional sentence was handed down, to be carried out after his four years had been served. Clearly, Henri could not be allowed free reign in France any longer, given the constant repetition of the very same crimes that he was so intent upon enacting, so it was decided that he should be exiled at the end of his four-year sentence. He was to be transported to the French Pacific Colony of New Caledonia on the opposite side of the world, where there would be neither the money nor infrastructure for him to carry out similar crimes again in the future.

The jail time was considered to be quite acceptable by Marie and the children, nothing more than father dearest deserved, but the sentence of transportation and exile was another matter. If Henri were exiled from France, they would never see him again, and perhaps more importantly, they would never see a penny of the vast fortune that they felt he owed them. It had been a difficult journey, coming to terms with the fact that Henri was a criminal, but it would have been rendered worthwhile if he were to slip a few francs into the pockets of his children every once in a while. If he was sent away, they would never see him again, and never get what they were owed.

Jeanne Cuchet was a seamstress. A markedly pretty woman in her late thirties who had been tragically widowed at a young age in 1909. By all accounts, her prospects of a second marriage should not have been terrible but for the fact that her son Andre, at the age of seventeen, seemed to predate her first marriage by quite a few years. This air of impropriety carried over into her working life, as she was an exceptionally talented maker of lingerie for one of the premier dressmakers in Paris. A product that everyone wanted, but nobody wished to acknowledge the manufacture of.

She had more or less given up on love when Raymond Diard came into her life by happenstance. A wealthy industrialist from Northern France, he had won her over rather simply with the promise of a future untarnished by shame and the prospect for her son to come to adulthood without the shadow of her indiscretions hanging over him. If they were wed and moved away from Paris, as Raymond insisted that they must, then it would be a fresh start for her and Andre. With some persuasion, Raymond parted her from her job and carried her off into the countryside to begin anew. In the village of Chantilly, some fifty miles north of Paris, he kept a small villa where they would be able to live together in comfort, all three of them. Andre mostly seemed to be stuck carrying the bags as his mother went through the motions – as though this were the grand romance of her lifetime rather than a last-minute attempt to course-correct.

Things went well for them in the beginning. They seemed relatively content in their lives. The only real point of contention in the little freshly-made family unit was Andre's fixation upon joining the army. His mother was desperate to keep him out, having heard the many horror stories from the front lines, but the boy had grown up with the romantic fantasies of honourable combat and men proving their worth, and he wanted it for himself. He wanted glory and he wanted to serve his country. As a veteran himself, Raymond was able to talk the boy down a little, pointing out that much of the daily life of a soldier was not actually exciting, but digging latrines and counting beans. Yet it became clear to Jeanne that he was not the ideal ally, as she often heard him telling her boy ribald tales, to their mutual amusement, about the various exploits of the young soldiers in training camp. On the one hand, she was pleased that her new beau was making such efforts to befriend the boy, but on the other, it was clearly doing nothing to abate the boy's hunger to run off and throw himself into the meat grinder at the earliest opportunity. Andre had already tried to join the army ahead of his scheduled recruitment date, and while his mother was trying to run out the clock on the war currently unfolding in Europe, he seemed intent on flinging himself directly into the heart of it.

She was not certain if there was an element of jealousy to it on the part of Raymond. Perhaps he wanted the boy out of the way so that he could have the mother's undivided attention at all times. If that were the case, it would explain the solution that he concocted. He found a job for Andre, working in a factory machining parts that would be used in the war effort. So important was this job that when the time came for his scheduled recruitment, they could make an argument that his current role in the war effort was too vital to send him out into the field. The boy was of course delighted that he could still contribute to the fight against the Germans while he waited for his opportunity to get out there, and Raymond had Jeanne all to himself in their little villa in the country.

Still, he was not a jailor to her there, he had to travel sometimes for his work, and he did not demand that she remain out in the country like she was some harem slave awaiting the return of her master. He arranged travel to Paris for her, ensured that she was comfortable staying with her sister, and then departed with promises of his imminent return.

Jeanne was of course terribly upset when Raymond did not come to collect her as expected, but her sister and her brother-in-law offered her words of comfort – with the war raging on, they reasoned, there was going to be some disruption of travel, she need not fear the worst so soon.

As the days drew on, however, a cold fear did begin to settle upon Jeanne. There was a war raging not so far to the east, a war that very well could have consumed poor Raymond if he had strayed too far afield. She did not like to think of what it would mean for her and her son if the man was dead. Nor did she truly like to think that Raymond himself had come to harm. She would admit to her sister that there was some part of her that was using Raymond for all the opportunities that he would bring her in life, but a far larger part had truly fallen for his charms.

He wasn't a handsome man, but by God did he make her laugh. When he spoke, it was as though the rest of the world faded away to background noise and just the two of them were in the room. Perhaps it was love, the kind of love that they wrote songs and poems about. Perhaps she had found the love of her life after so very much of her life had already been lived. Fate would not be so cruel as to snatch him from her now, would it?

Dreading the worst and becoming increasingly hysterical with each passing day, it was finally agreed that she, Andre, and her brother-in-law should travel to the villa in Chantilly to see if there was any evidence to be found as to her missing lover's location. Even something as simple as a receipt for a train ticket might tell them where to begin their search for the missing man.

They arrived in the dim early hours of the evening to find the house looking entirely abandoned. There was no sign that Raymond had returned in their absence, or that the gate had even been opened since their departure for Paris. It should have been another shard of ice thrust through poor Jeanne's heart, but she moved with a determination now that shocked her son. She had decided that she was not willing to simply stand back and allow fate to carry her wherever it may. She was an active player in her own tale, she would track her Raymond down and she would not believe that he was dead until she held his bones, because she knew finally in that moment – while standing on the threshold of the dead and silent villa, that she loved him. She did. All of this time she had wondered about and second-guessed her own intentions, but the gaping dark pit in her heart, the agony that she was experiencing at the thought that her Raymond might be dead and forever gone; that was the evidence that she had been lacking.

Inside the house, she swiftly lit lamps for the men and sent them about hunting. Raymond had desks and cupboards all over the place, he was a collector of antiques, but he did not let them sit idle. Every piece of furniture served its purpose in the vast filing system of his home, though if asked, it was likely he could never have told anyone how that system worked – only that when he needed something he knew where to look for it. The controlled chaos of it all worked perfectly for him, but it made it impossible for Jeanne and her son to know where to even begin looking. They hauled open every door, cracked open every chest, checked anywhere that there might have been any clue as to what had become of Raymond. They searched with ferocity through the night.

But in the cold light of dawn, when the evidence they had gathered was laid out before them, it made no sense. There was no clear sign of where Raymond had gone, nor any suggestion as to where his factories in the north of France were located. He had certainly acquired the deeds to many pieces of property, but almost all were small residential ones rather than the vast industrial spaces he must have required for manufacturing. Furthermore, when they examined his accounting, where they'd hoped to find some past record of spending that might have indicated where he spent his time while travelling, they instead, discovered a complicated and confusing hodge-podge of dozens upon dozens of different incomes. They had found what looked like army pensions for other men being paid into Raymond's accounts. They had found what looked like widows' pensions being paid into other accounts that he controlled, not to mention the books for multiple businesses that Raymond had never even mentioned. Most damning of all, however, were the identity documents that her brother-in-law had uncovered. The name upon those papers was not that of Raymond Diard, but of a Henri Landru. At first, she tried to set it aside as a mistake, but again and again, the name appeared on numerous documents. Many of the accounts that Raymond accessed had Landru's name upon them, along with a host of other unfamiliar names. It would have taken a forensic accountant months to decipher what they had discovered in that one frantic night, but they were not in Chantilly trying to find evidence of wrongdoing. They were desperately searching for some hint of where the man might be found. So when it was discovered that Raymond, or Henri, or whatever his name really was, had an apartment that he still owned in Paris, that was where the investigating trio headed next.

And it was there that Raymond was truly to be damned.

The Cuchets discovered Henri Landru's true identity when they attempted to gain access to the newly discovered apartment in Paris. The police confronted them shortly after their unsuccessful attempt, and as Jeanne told her story of a lost love, the expression on the faces of the gendarmes became increasingly sympathetic – they recognized many of the hallmarks of Landru's previous schemes. They asked her if Raymond Diard had requested money to invest, or if he'd urged her to sign over her pension – or anything of the sort. She was enraged at the implication. Raymond was not some petty crook trying to trick her, he was the love of her life, a businessman who had gone missing, and instead of investigating that and helping her like they were meant to, the police were instead choosing to spin nonsense tales connecting him to some conman. It was everything that she had already suspected and feared, from the moment that her 'too-good-to-be-true' lover had appeared to begin with. And it made her very uncomfortable.

The final damning blow that the police left Jeanne with was the knowledge that if Raymond or Henri or whoever he was passing himself off as nowadays was spotted in Paris, he was to be immediately deported to New Caledonia, to serve out the remainder of his years. He was guilty of terrible crimes and had been convicted and sentenced for them. This was a man on the run from justice. With the full weight of all this laid upon her, the police had hoped that Jeanne would crumble and hand over what information she had on Raymond's location, but she was stalwart in the face of all the evidence. She would hear it all from Raymond, and then make her decision. Just as soon as she could find him.

Her brother-in-law had understandably abandoned the search for Raymond at this juncture, fully convinced by the words of the police and the ample evidence that he had seen in Chantilly that something was amiss with regard to Jeanne's new beau. Her sister helped her establish herself in Paris with a new apartment and some odd jobs as a seamstress. Despite her sister's and brother-in-law's best efforts to help Jeanne get back on her feet and on with her life, it seemed that Jeanne had no desire to get on with her life. At least not without Raymond. She wanted Raymond back.

The longer Raymond was absent, the more withdrawn she became - until her sister no longer heard from her at all. Even Andre, who could usually be relied upon to pull his mother out of her funk and drag her back into the family that existed rather than the one that she'd imagined for herself, had lost touch with his aunt and uncle. He seemed to be making no effort to stay in contact, despite how lenient they'd been regarding him being born on the wrong side of the sheets. The radio silence continued when Andre abruptly quit his job in the factory and he and Jeanne both disappeared from Paris entirely. Nobody could work out the exact date they had vanished, or if they had vanished at all. In all the chaos of the time, they could very well have travelled by normal means, sending letters to let others know of their location, and the mail had gotten lost. There was no way to know for certain. What did seem certain was that in the month before they departed from Paris, there was a spring in Jeanne's step again. The reunited pseudo-family made their home in another peripheral village within easy reach of Paris – this time Vernouillet, a scant twenty miles up the River Seine that runs through Paris itself. Henri was now introducing himself, and signing the documentation, as Henri Cuchet, having adopted himself into the family in his fiction. The little cottage that they rented in Vernouillet was in that name, and everyone in the village treated them as a true family, rather than people to be looked down upon and detested. Andre became Henri's son in all aspects, except being party to the truth about his new father.

Jeanne and Andre began writing letters to friends back in Paris, calming tensions, and calling off search parties. Jeanne's family had suspected that she might still be involved with the rapscallion Landru and would have warned her off resuming her relationship with the silver-tongued swindler. but by making out as though she had a new beau who had already wed her, the situation was entirely different.

Her friends were delighted for her, and many wished to visit, but by the time communication had resumed, it was already heading into winter. As such, Jeanne begged off visitors, citing the awful weather that they were having out in the country. Mud as high as her knees. She told them to wait until spring. They would all be reunited in joy then.

Similarly, Andre put off any visits back to town with his mates from the factory by claiming that he wouldn't be around long enough to make it worthwhile. His new stepfather had pulled some strings with old army buddies and secured him early acceptance into the armed forces. Before they could get out to the village, he'd already be gone to fight the brutish German invaders.

The letters went on for many weeks, back and forth, and then, abruptly, the Cuchets stopped replying. At first, it was discounted as disrupted mail due to the war, or perhaps the bad weather that Jeanne had spoken of. Having lived all of their lives in Paris, many of their social circle had no real grasp of the distances to anywhere outside of the city. When Jeanne had announced the location of her new home, it may as well have been on the moon to most of them, though she had claimed she'd still be able to visit frequently. Gradually, it became apparent that Jeanne and her son had gone missing once more. Finally, sufficient pressure had mounted for the police to send a gendarme out to the village to look for them.

In Vernouillet, the police heard tales of the happy family, settling into life in the cottage, keeping to themselves for the most part, but not to an unsociable degree. They had seemed pleasant enough and then they had departed to parts unknown. The husband had paid up rent for many months in advance stating the intention of returning soon before he, too, had departed the village. A cursory check of the cottage showed no signs of anything untoward, so the police considered the whole thing to be a misunderstanding and assumed that the Cuchet family would be back in touch with their friends at a later date.

Their bones had been burned in the fireplace of the cottage after they had been murdered, the bodies butchered down into pieces before their impromptu cremations. Gradually, Henri had worked his way up from the feet, portioning one part of his lover and her son into the flames at a time, until finally there was nothing left of them. Then he swept out all of the ashes and bone shards and scattered them across the garden. The remains would never be found, and the only way that we know that this is how the bodies were disposed of is through circumstantial evidence and comments made long after the fact.

There were a great many reasons that Henri Landru might have murdered the two of them. An argument may have sprung up regarding one of his myriad lies, or perhaps some unknown aspect of his true life had been brought to light that he did not want to discuss. It may be that an argument escalated to the point of physical violence, after which it was easier to continue with the violence rather than dealing with the consequences. It could have been the little pebble on the slippery slope that sent Henri Landru sliding down into the history books instead of fading into obscurity. However, this seems inconsistent with his character.

Henri Landru was never an angry man. He was never the kind of man who would allow his emotions to control him. Whatever else he may have despised about his father, the stoic self-control that the big man had possessed had passed down to his son, who made all of his decisions based on logic rather than gut feeling. If Henri was to become a killer, it would not have been due to some foolish argument getting out of hand, or some flare-up of anger at his lies being discovered and confronted. His entire history shows us that when caught in a lie, Henri would simply concoct another to explain why he had lied, to begin with. Even when he was caught red-handed, he would have an excuse prepared. There is a strong argument to be made that his faux suicide attempt in prison was an attempt to set precedent for insanity pleas further down the line, even though he suspected that the initial one was doomed to failure. He was a meticulous man who planned out everything in the finest detail, and if he ever appeared to be flustered or flat-footed, it was only because he had chosen to appear so.

Far more likely, Henri had killed the Cuchets because he simply had no more use for them.

It had been fun for him to play at being a father and husband again, it had satisfied him to go through those motions. He had felt good about his pretty new wife and his proud new son. They had been a distraction for him while he waited for the situation in Paris to calm down. But now they had reached the end of their usefulness. They were generating more problems than they were solving. The return on the investment of his time was no longer profitable.

It was not as though he would have struggled to find another pretty woman to play house with when the mood took him, not even one with a grown son if he suddenly decided that aspect of the game was what interested him. Jeanne Cuchet had filled a role in his little fantasy, and when he no longer required her for that purpose he had made a decision.

Previously, he had ended these affairs with abandonment, pure and simple. Seducing women for what he wanted from them, whether that was love, money, or simply the sense of victory that he derived from tricking them. When he had gotten what he wanted and was finished with them, he would simply move on to the next target. But something had changed in his mental calculus. On balance, leaving behind a woman who might tell tales was no longer an acceptable risk. Too much evidence against him could result in his eventual capture, arrest, and deportation. The stakes had been raised, and he needed to manipulate events more completely to ensure the outcomes that he desired would come to pass.

He could no longer afford to leave behind bereft and penniless widows to run and tell their tales to the police. He could no longer seduce women for the enjoyment of their bodies, walk away laughing, and expect them not to use every detail they knew about him against him. There had been sufficient evidence provided to him that his previous behaviour was reckless, therefore he modified his behaviour to make himself immune to the errors of the past. If he left nobody in his wake to stand witness, there would be no evidence against him. If he had just slit the throat of the stupid widow he'd tricked out of her inheritance, then he'd never have had to deal with jail time at all.

To an outside observer, it may have seemed like a reckless leap all on its own to go from fraud to murder, but once the moral boundary had been crossed, Henri no longer made any distinctions. Surely there was something of a flaw in the black-and-white thinking that all sin was treated as equal, as he had been raised to believe. There were no lesser or greater evils in the Landru household, only the righteous and the sinners, nothing in between. So, when Henri made the active choice to step over that line, he knew that there was no going back, and no point in considering himself the moral superior of anyone just because their crimes differed.

Regardless of why he elected to kill the pair, the fact remained that he had done so. Any remaining moral horizon had been crossed, and murder had now become part of the repertoire of solutions that he could apply to a problem. And Henri had no shortage of loose ends that he needed to preemptively tie off before they had the chance to incriminate him.

The Road to Gambais

Henri arrived back in Paris the same day that he departed Vernouillet, long before the first inklings of suspicion had begun to build up. Along the way he had paused only to send off a completed but, as yet, unsent letter from his now-dead adoptive son to an uncle. His plan was to provide himself with the widest possible window before any real attempt was made to look for them. He had left no evidence behind at the cottage, but that did not mean he wanted the police poking around anywhere near him if it could be avoided.

On his return, he went immediately to his wife's side. Throughout his latest absence, they had of course remained in correspondence as they always did when he departed the city. Marie may have become more aware of her husband's flaws as the years went by, and he picked her pocket again and again, but he was still her husband, and she still had that diagnosis from a court doctor to use as a talisman to ward off any unpleasant thoughts she had about him not even loving her, and just using her.

When he came bearing gifts, it was enough of a surprise to knock the wind out of her sails before she could even begin laying into him for the latest bout of spousal abandonment. A beautiful necklace, fancier than anything she'd ever known.

He claimed that he'd seen it and immediately pictured it around her neck. He hadn't been able to stay away, from the moment he found that gift for her, he had felt compelled to rush home and give it to her because just that momentary thought of her was all it had taken to make him long for the love of his life once more.

And like the desperate fool she was, she believed him and clasped the chain behind her neck, and wore dead Jeanne Cuchet's jewellery until the police finally snatched it off her years later for use as evidence.

Henri did not kill his wife, he kept her sweet. She had entirely too much value to him as a resource while he was out of town, tracking events and keeping him informed, and more importantly, the ties between them were too obvious and too public. It was one thing to quietly dispose of one of his random women, but to kill Marie just so that he didn't need to deal with her anymore would have led the police directly to his door.

Their relationship may have briefly seemed as though it were on the mend after this latest return to the city, but both of them knew it couldn't last. Not when he was a wanted man.

Thérèse Laborde-Line was a divorced, unemployed widow in a time when any one of those things would have made her a social pariah. She had originated in Argentina before relocating from the colony to France itself early in her life, and it had always marked her as somewhat exotic to straight-laced Parisian society. She had one son, a postal clerk, from whom she was now quite thoroughly estranged, and no other contact with the outside world to speak of.

Left with few options, she had posted an advertisement, offering herself up as a lady's companion, with the hope that some well-off woman somewhere in France might require someone to do her hair and dress her in exchange for room and board. But with no employment history for providing such services and no résumé to speak of, she had very slim hopes of receiving an answer.

In May of 1915, a letter arrived with her name on it, not from some rich woman who couldn't be bothered to dress herself, but from a man of means, who hoped to undress her instead.

Henri was not quite so forward as that in his letter to her, responding to her search for work as though he were simply offering a different position to her, rather than treating her job application as a lonely-hearts column. Explaining his own situation, as a man in need of companionship, looking for a woman of a similar age that he might wed. He explained that many of the same tasks as would have been required of her as a lady's companion might still be required of her. She would have to make conversation and sometimes serve tea if they had guests, and there was also the possibility for their relationship to be considerably more intimate than that between employer and employee, though he would of course furnish her with whatever income she required to be comfortable, or rather, he would share his own income with her, as if she were his wife.

This was in fact the entirety of the job role. To keep house, manage the household accounts, dine in company, and to provide him with the kind of companionship that he had been craving since the death of his own wife.

It was an extremely familiar ruse at this point in his career as a trickster. He had a great many single women "on the hook" at any given moment, teasing each of them closer and closer to actually meeting up with him, at which point he overwhelmed them with gifts and charm and closed the deal. Victory was what he craved more than the carnal release that he implied he was seeking, and he would take that victory either in their submission to him or in his ability to steal from them. Either way, he was able to dominate them, and this pleased him immensely.

Thérèse was not immediately taken in, she was older and wiser than many of his previous victims, more accustomed to a world where kindness was a pleasant dream and cruelty the abundant reality. Yet he grew on her as they corresponded back and forth. He was well versed in the right thing to say at the right time by this point in his career as a serial seducer, and it did not take long before she consented to meet him for a dinner date, here and there.

There was no pressure from him, which seemed incongruous with his interest in her, and incongruous with how any sort of con artist might have behaved. He did not pursue her with the wild abandon of a younger man but was steady in his course. Arranging dates when they were suitable to their schedules and remaining respectful in his behaviour, despite his professed interest in her. It verged upon mysterious, and despite her experience in the arena of love, Thérèse was nonetheless afflicted with the same desire to solve a mystery that affects all of us. She became the pursuer, and when he finally succumbed to her advances, she felt a genuine sense of victory.

They travelled together to a little cottage that he kept outside of the city so that they might experiment a little with what life might be like for the two of them if they were to make their coupling official. Vernouillet was little changed since Henri had last departed it, and while a few of the villagers might have seen Mr Cuchet arriving with a woman who was not his wife, none of them were intimate enough with the family to feel any need to intervene on her behalf.

Marriages failed, even in those days when a failed marriage was considered a massive moral failing too. And with the war raging and all the world in flux, there was no saying with certainty what had become of the previous relationship. Indeed, given how eager his young son had been to go off to war, it was not difficult to imagine scenarios that might have ended the marriage in tragedy. So if he meant to start anew, who would begrudge him that?

Thérèse was never seen again, and it would be a great many months before anyone commented upon her absence from Paris. Even her son, when made aware of her unexplained departure from the city had little interest in tracking her down. Why would he? She was an embarrassment to him and his young wife. If she were gone it could only make his life easier.

Once again, oily black smoke poured from the chimney of the cottage in Vernouillet. Once again, he scattered ashes and fragments of bone across the gardens. His new wife was nowhere to be seen, and it would not be long before Henri Cuchet departed from the village once more, too.

While he had been entertaining Thérèse, Henri had not been idle elsewhere. His funds were rapidly depleting once more, thanks to the extravagant lifestyle he liked to live to impress his new women, so he knew that logically, the next victim he took would need to provide something in the way of a monetary injection instead of merely providing him with the satisfaction of victory.

In May 1915, at the same time as his courtship of Thérèse, he had placed a memo in the lonely-hearts column of Le Journal, a popular Parisian paper of the time, targeting women of a certain age and station.

He positioned himself in the somewhat unbelievable role of the new Consul-General to Australia, claiming that he required a competent wife to host at diplomatic functions, preferably one who had previously been a professional in some capacity, or at least capable of managing a substantial household. He had, in essence, taken the part of his real life in which he was condemned to deportation to the southern hemisphere, and woven it into the dense thicket of lies that he led all of his unfortunate victims into.

This business of advertising for a wife the way one would a personal assistant may seem terribly unorthodox by today's standards, but at the time, such advertisements were more or less standard should an adult man find himself in need of a wife. A marriage was as much a business transaction to be negotiated as it was a love match, with the former part often being considered vastly more important than the latter, at least in the higher echelons of society. By placing such an advert, Henri eliminated all of the lower class, lower income contenders, leaving only a crop of wealthy older women who he could freely prey upon.

Women such as Marie-Angélique Guillin. Marie-Angélique was in her fifties, widowed, and a retired housekeeper. Her previous employers, in life, had adored her, as she had run such a well-kept home for them. When they passed from the mortal coil around 1910, they left behind a substantial inheritance for her as a way of thanks so that she would never again have to undertake such heavy labour in her later years. After a life of service, Marie-Angélique felt that she was entitled to a better life now that she had retired. She had nobody left in Paris, no friends, no family, and even her old employers were now gone, so the prospect of starting over somewhere new and exotic like Australia was incredibly appealing to her.

When they met, it was equal parts date and job interview. After only a short time talking, the formalities were dropped, and Henri announced himself to be thoroughly enthralled with Marie-Angélique. She was of course flattered, but not ready to make any sort of commitment at that very early juncture. Being the absolute gentleman that he was, Henri immediately backed off to give her the space that she needed, reverting to a more laid-back approach that seemed to run contrary to the passion he had shown but a moment before. It confused Marie-Angélique sufficiently that she put some further distance between them. Even though he had a fixed deadline when he meant to depart France and travel to the far side of the world, she asked him to delay, to give her the time that she needed to make up her mind. And to her utter amazement, he did.

He would hold off on travelling all the way around the world, just so that he might have her company. If there were anything that might have convinced her of his truthfulness, it was that. Marie-Angélique consented to be his wife, and so he made arrangements with her for a sort of trial run before they made their lengthy trek to the southern hemisphere. This way she could make sure that she was content in his company when it was not just a fleeting visit, and that she was up to the fairly simple tasks that would be expected of her once he was at the consulate. For this purpose, they travelled out to one of his properties in the village of Vernouillet, a little cottage that he kept, mostly as a place to store those parts of his collection of antiques that were not going to be shipped overseas.

There certainly was a hodgepodge nature to the home when they arrived, and it took Henri no small amount of time to clear some wardrobe space for all of Marie-Angélique's dresses. The place did not look nearly so fine as she would have expected from a gentleman of Henri's standing, but she supposed that one never looked their best while in the process of travelling to the opposite side of the planet.

She had uprooted her entire life to come here, as a stepping stone towards what she hoped would become her future, withdrawing every penny from her accounts with the full expectation that she would never return to France again.

Henri was, of course, aware of this, having made many suggestions and hints to that effect in their conversations, priming her to carry out the actions that he required her to carry out, without actually telling her to do anything at all. It had been subtle enough, little hints that he didn't care much for women who brought nothing to the relationship. Suggestions that he would begrudge handling every petty penny that had to be traded to keep his household running. Nothing substantial enough that she could hold it against him, but just enough to make her think that life would be easier if she had her own funds to draw on for the little things in life instead of having to go begging Henri with her cap in hand every time they needed some milk. She was pretty sure he'd even mentioned knowing a chap who could exchange any Francs that she had into Australian money at a good rate. She was sure he'd said that in passing. Another little seed planted, slowly germinating to fruition. Henri was a capable manipulator, and with time he had gone from simply overwhelming his victims with charisma and love-bombing to more complex modes of behavioural control. His pattern of behaviour may not have changed, but the tools that he used to achieve his goals had grown with him.

It was several days into their stay in Vernouillet before Marie-Angélique finally allowed herself to be seduced. She had been patient, weighing the odds of every outcome, judging Henri's every word and action, but at last, she was convinced that his commitment was too grand now for him to back out and abandon her if she gave herself over to him.

Henri fell upon her like a ravenous beast after being on his best behaviour for so long during his seduction of her, and she found herself teetering upon the precipice of actually falling in love with the man, so deep ran his passions for her.

Yet the next day, he seemed changed. He was smugly self-satisfied as many men seemed to be after the culmination of their lusts, but it was more than that. All of the affectations that she had taken to be his personality had abruptly disappeared. When she tried to talk to him, he was dismissive. When she tried to discuss their plans for the future, he asked her directly about the money that she had inherited, and where it was, as he planned to change their francs for Australian pounds. She had never mentioned her inheritance to him in any direct terms, so this sudden change of subject left her startled and confused. She gave away the location of the compartment of her chest where she had hidden all of her cash, and he was off like a shot out of a gun digging through her belongings until he found it, throwing her clothes and undergarments about like confetti while she tried half-heartedly to stop him. Finally, she struck him on the cheek when he would give her no acknowledgement, and at last, he froze in place. The money crumpled up in his hands. He set it down again and then turned to give Marie-Angélique his full attention.

She would be the last woman to die in the cottage in Vernouillet. Henri's comings and goings as Mr Cuchet had drawn too much attention from the locals, and he had no intention of getting caught because of something so silly. Oily black smoke poured from the cottage chimney as he went about packing up those valuables that were portable enough to carry off, and he made arrangements with the landlord the next day, after scattering ashes over the gardens, for the remaining furniture to be sold along in lieu of his final month's rent as he claimed that he would be moving abroad to join his wife in their new home in one of the colonies.

He had secured enough walking around money that it would be possible to easily establish a new base of operations, and he chose a villa in the village of Gambais, for which he would later become infamous, to make his new home.

It was better appointed than his cottage in Vernoiuillet, with more space for those various antiques and collectables he had decided to cart there from their storage in Paris, and it was further out from the nearest village, granting a degree more privacy than he had enjoyed at his previous country home. It also featured a substantial cast-iron stove as its primary source of heating, which he now considered to be an essential. The entire place was set up to his exacting standards, for a very specific purpose. Now that he had the specific pattern of his crimes worked out, all that he needed were more victims, and he had no shortage of possibilities in that regard. The lonely-hearts columns were always awaiting new letters and Paris, in a time of war, was overflowing with women bereft of their beaus. Henri had his pick of the crop.

Bluebeard's Castle

Henri had met his next victim in Le Havre during his exile there in 1915, but at the time she was already married. They had remained in contact throughout the years, with intermittent letters passing back and forth between them, but no real push towards a culmination of their relationship. Hers was only one of the great many lines that Henri kept in the water at any given time. His correspondence must have been a full-time job in itself.

Berthe Héon had lost her husband in the intervening years, after which she had taken a new lover, who had also died recently. Her two children from the marriage had died in the war, and to top it all off, her beloved illegitimate daughter whom she had conceived with her now-dead lover had recently passed away too, in childbirth. It had been an endless cavalcade of miseries for years, one horror after another, wearing Berthe down until she could scarcely even stomach getting out of bed in the morning. Her life was over. Her hopes for the future were destroyed. Yet still, she was here.

In the middle of the summer of 1915, while between the Cuchet family and Marie-Angélique, Henri had remade her acquaintance when she moved to Paris in search of work as a cleaner. She was flat broke by this point, desperate for anything to take the awful weight of trying to keep herself alive off her shoulders when she wasn't even certain that she wanted to be alive at all.

Henri was a shoulder for her to cry on at first. An old friend who had crossed paths with her after far too long. A missed connection that was finally being made. He was always too busy for their relationship to actually progress, but in their brief moments together, he was always a perfect gentleman, charming and kind, insisting on paying for everything. It was precisely what Berthe needed. Someone to take control over her life, to give her a purpose and direction. She knew that he was a businessman with a more than healthy income and that he had some grand plans for the future, but it was only towards the end of the year that he finally sat down with her and laid out what those plans were.

He meant to travel around the world to start fresh in the "pretty colony" of Tunisia, but he did not want to make that journey alone. They had been friends for a very long time, and now he hoped that they might take their relationship a little further. If they could become lovers before he departed France forever, then he would take her as his bride and carry her off with him. She too could start her life over in the sun, leaving behind the cruel pangs of her past and beginning to live again for herself. The poverty and hardship she experienced now would become nothing but a dim memory in the colonies, where she would be waited on by the natives and serve as mistress of a grand household. It was more than Berthe could ever have hoped for, and by this point in her life, she had already abandoned all hope. If he was lying to her, then her life could not possibly get any worse than it already was, and if he was being truthful, then all the wrongs of the past could be left on this side of the ocean.

They fell into bed together at some point during Henri's seduction of Marie-Angélique, while the wealthy woman was still resisting his advances, and Henri could not have been a more exciting lover. He felt like an exotic visitor from another world as he dropped into her dingy little apartment all dressed up in his nice suits and ties. Berthe fell for him more with every passing visit, and finally – after he had disposed of the bodies of his previous victims – he came to her and invited her to come and live with him. Not in Tunisia, not yet, but in one of his houses in the country, where they could play as husband and wife for a while until they felt certain that this new aspect of their relationship was sustainable, and until his new estate in Tunisia had been built to his specifications.

She was the first of a great many women to visit Henri in Gambais, and one of the few who was witnessed arriving. She had little in the way of luggage, but Henri assured her that was for the best. When they made the journey to Tunisia, the clothes that she wore here in France would be entirely inappropriate. He would far rather she travel light, and he could pay for her to have a new wardrobe made on their arrival. She had little choice in the matter of course. She was destitute.

All that she had left, after a lifetime of hardships and sorrow was her own life. Only the beating of her heart, and the memories of those that she had lost to carry on into the future. Henri took even that from her. When he grew bored with the limited entertainment that she could provide him, he could quite easily have parted ways with her amicably. They had a long history as friends, and as beaten down as Berthe had been by the world, she likely would have accepted this latest abandonment as her due. Instead, he chose to choke the life out of her, carve her body up into small pieces, and incinerate those pieces in the big cast iron wood-burning stove.

Once she was reduced to bone fragments and ashes, he scattered them across the gardens of his new villa. As jovial as if nothing more untoward was happening than a little bit of out-of-season fertilising.

It would be almost a year later before Henri took another victim that we know about.

It was at about this time that Henri's elder son Maurice was arrested. He had been mobilised to join the battle against the Germans in 1915 but conducted a side business as a fence for stolen goods in his downtime. – primarily selling off the belongings of Jeanne Cuchet that had somehow come into his possession. Henri did what he could to help his son, putting him in touch with the best of the lawyers that had represented him in the past, but it was of no use, and the young soldier served several years of jail time.

In the meantime, Charles, his youngest son became Henri's self-styled apprentice, picking up all the details of his father's work so that he could take over himself when he was fully grown. Serving as his chauffeur when he was in the city, and his go-between in the sale of stolen goods when his father was out of town. Charles also served as Henri's hands within the city, when his father had to remain out of sight. He showed up to the apartments of many of his father's victims, let himself in, and gathered up anything of resale value, to maximise the profit from each and every killing.

Anna Collomb was a typist at an insurance company in Paris. She was sharp-witted and charming, as well as being widely described by those who knew her as attractive. At forty-four years old, she was widowed and had few good prospects. After the death of her bankrupt and alcoholic husband, she had spent a great deal of time attempting to claw her way back out of the hole that he had dug for her. She had taken on a string of younger lovers, expecting each one of them, in turn, to marry her and put her life back into order, but none seemed interested in pursuing the relationship to that point, only up to the point that they had their needs satisfied.

As a result of one lover's satisfaction, Anna had been left with a daughter, an illegitimate child who would have proved her ruin if she bandied her around town like some of the shameless and wanton women of Paris. Instead, she took after her Catholic forebearers and sent the child off to be raised in a nunnery in Italy rather than live with the shame. She was another one of those who answered Henri's lonely-hearts advertisement, probably hoping that Henri would serve as a stepfather to her bastard child and that they could form a family once more. After a few dates in Paris, she travelled out to stay at his chateau in the country, planning on wintering there. She would never return.

In April of 1917, we come across the next victim that we know about, Andrée Babelay. Andrée was entirely different from any of Henri's prior victims. At only nineteen years old, she was decades younger than the women that he usually targeted. Technically she was employed, sporadically, as a nanny by various families in Paris, but she made the majority of her income through prostitution. Henri had engaged her services once or twice through the years and bumped into her by chance on the metro one evening in Paris. She called out to him across the train with the pet name she had invented for him "Lulu."

Deciding that it was fate, the two of them travelled together to his apartment near the Gare du Nord where they drank and chatted all through the night, entirely enamoured with one another's company. Andrée was completely different from his other victims in many respects, the foremost of which was not her age, or her profession, but her vivaciousness. She lit up every room that she entered and basked in the attention that she received. She was quick and witty, matching Henri's charms perfectly in ways that his usually slow-witted prey could not. She served as both a challenge and entertainment for Henri, and he found that he did not desire to part ways with her. As such, they spent a few days together in that apartment in Paris before travelling together once more to his villa in Gambais.

Few of the women who came out to stay with Henri were ever seen once they had arrived, and the vast majority came and vanished without anyone in the village being any the wiser. Henri himself came and went freely without anyone taking notice either. So the fact that there is a written record of Andrée's time in Gambais is something quite remarkable. More remarkable still is what the local game warden spotted her and Henri doing out in the woods.

He was teaching her how to ride a bicycle.

The relationship between the two of them, already muddied by her profession and his murderous past, took a turn for the bizarre as he treated the young prostitute as much like an adoptive daughter as he ever did a lover. The kisses that he was seen planting upon her were considered chaste, even by the conservative-minded folk of the village of Gambais.

The relationship was never clarified, for the game warden, or any of the people in the village he told about the odd sight, because the next time Henri was spotted abroad, he was alone once more. The woman he had been with, whether she was a lover, niece, or something else had vanished from existence like so many of the women in his life. No trace of her was ever found, no friends in Paris ever heard from her again. It was as though she had vanished into thin air. Her Lulu, on the other hand, persisted.

Célestine Buisson was a return to form for Henri. Another unfortunate who had answered his 1915 lonely-hearts posting, though it was a full two years later before their relationship began to take strides forward. Célestine was a widowed housekeeper of about fifty years, who became lonely after her adult son was mobilised to join the armed forces countering the German advance. She was a very naïve soul compared to most of the women that Henri pursued, and rather homely in appearance, leading many to speculate that he was only after her for her money. Yet it came as a surprise to many who suspected that there was foul play afoot that Henri, or Georges Frémyet as he was known to Célestine, seemed to be in no hurry to close the deal and lay his hands on her money.

In fact, while they became engaged in 1915, wedding plans moved at a glacially slow pace, with Georges making myriad excuses for the slow progress and Célestine pushing constantly to set a date. At first, he was travelling abroad on business, then, when he returned, some of his personal documents were found to have been lost – presumably held by one of the foreign visa agencies that he had been working with to facilitate safe transit through war-torn Europe. It took a full two years before he was able to fully commit to the wedding, with all of his paperwork finally organised, and even then, he seemed intent upon having a dry run of the marriage first, inviting Célestine out to his villa in Gambais so that they might live together a while and discuss all of the details.

She travelled out to Gambais with her half-sister in tow. Her half-sister, Marie Lacoste, had serious reservations about Célestine's marriage, and in her meetings with Georges at Célestine's apartment in France his charms had done little to win her over. She was convinced that he was some sort of confidence trickster, intent on defrauding Célestine of her savings, something that seemed to be confirmed for her when they arrived in Gambais and she learned that Georges had apparently been managing her half-sister's investments for over a year already. Georges took a step back, choosing not to insert himself into what he considered to be a family matter. He had no need to. Célestine was already primed and ready to go to war on his behalf.

She and Marie argued incessantly about the matter for the duration of their stay in Gambais, and by the time that the two of them took a train back to Paris together, neither was on speaking terms with the other. Marie had essentially announced that it was Georges or her, and Célestine, ever the romantic, had chosen her fiancé. If she was so intent on ruining herself, Marie had no choice but to leave her to her foolishness. But she waited each day with bated breath to receive the inevitable letter begging her to come and bail

Célestine out once Georges had made off with all of her money and left her alone and destitute.

A day after their return to Paris, Célestine and Georges said their goodbyes and purchased a one-way train ticket back to Gambais, where they meant to make their home, leaving only a passing jab at Marie that she shouldn't wait for an invitation to their wedding.

That was the last time that Célestine Buisson was seen alive, but it was not the last that Marie would hear from her. Two separate letters arrived for her from her half-sister, seeking reconciliation and inviting her out to Gambais once more where Marie would be able to see for herself that all was well and everything had worked out for the best. But Marie truly was sharper than her half-sister and immediately recognised that the signatures at the end of each of these letters were forgeries.

For Henri, Marie Lacoste was an unbearable loose end that he desperately needed to tie off. He had been so very careful in the years after his imprisonment to ensure that he left nobody behind with bad feelings towards him, certain that they would come back to bite him at the most inopportune of moments. He paid off the lease on Célestine's apartment in Paris to maintain the illusion that she was still alive and when it became apparent that his attempts to lure Marie out to his killing den were not going to be successful, he switched tactics, showing up at her workplace and begging her to come to dinner at her half-sister's apartment so that the two of them might reconcile.

Already suspicious, and more than a little furious that Célestine was sending the man that she so detested to invite her, Marie refused his invitation twice, adding on the second time around that he should not come back again as he was stirring her to fresh anger over a matter she had hoped to leave settled.

Back in Célestine's apartment, all of the furniture and furnishings had been stripped out and sold. It was a bare, empty shell of the home it had once been, the perfect place for Henri to ambush Marie and put an end to her suspicions once and for all. She was not taken in by his lies, and so, she survived.

As for his own Marie, this is where she re-enters the story, as he needed someone to masquerade as Célestine to go and withdraw all of the money from her savings accounts.

Marie Landru did exactly what was asked of her, dressing up in Celestine's clothes, carrying all of her papers and telling precisely the lies that she had been told. She had no real understanding of what had happened to the previous owner of her outfit or the real owner of the accounts, assuming that this was just another of Henri's fraud victims. For her part in his crimes, she received as her reward an apartment in the northwestern suburb of Paris, under the assumed name of Mrs Marie Frémyet. Another one of Henri's aliases that was rapidly blossoming out into a whole person of its own.

Louise Jaume was the next of his victims. She was a devout Catholic woman who worked as an assistant dressmaker. Despite her devotion to the tenets of Catholicism and all of the rules that accompanied that devotion, she had recently filed for divorce from her estranged husband and become single as an adult for the first time in her life. She met with Henri, under his alias of Lucien Guillet after spotting his lonely-hearts advertisement in Paris' conservative newspaper and being intrigued by the story that he told there. According to his advertisement, Lucien was a refugee from the Ardennes region that had been occupied by the German forces and was attempting to make a new life for himself in central France. She was quite charmed by the man when she met him. His rather homely appearance convinced her that he was not some sort of playboy trying to pick up women easily, beguiling her into a false sense of security as their courtship dragged on. Despite his professed passion for her, Louise refused to engage in the kind of sordid behaviour that he was attempting to tempt her into, choosing instead to keep their relationship chaste until they were wed.

This presented something of a problem for Henri, as he had no intention of actually marrying anyone. He had no official documentation for his Lucien persona, so even if he had no issues with the idea of polygamy, it would have been impossible to pursue. As such he was at something of a dead end with Jaume for quite some time. Finally, he cottoned on to a means to subvert her expectations and break down her defences. He began attending mass with her regularly, convincing her that he too was still a good Catholic, despite all of the evidence to the contrary. Finally, he took her to a grand mass at the Basilica of Sacre Cœur and she was caught up in the finery and beauty of what was considered by many to be the greatest church in all of Paris. So convinced was she in that moment that she consented to take a trip with him, to visit his home in the village of Gambais, where he hoped that they might make a home together.

Whether or not their relationship was consummated on arrival to his little love nest villa is unknown, though Henri himself would later claim that it was. Regardless, the end result was the same. His hands tightening around her throat, her body condemned to the flames of his cast iron stove.

Marie Landru masqueraded as Louise when visiting a bank on Henri's behalf, clumsily forging the woman's signature when withdrawing all of her savings. She should, by all rights, have been caught in this deception, but it seemed that the bank clerk simply didn't double-check the signature against the one on file. An oversight that led to further deaths that could very well have been avoided.

Victorine Pellat sent a letter to the mayor of Gambais at about this time in 1917, inquiring after the health of her older sister Anna Collumb, who had moved to his prefecture with a gentleman she knew by the name of Cuchet. The mayor recognised the description of the man as someone else entirely, a Raoul Dupont, who rented the Maison Tric, a little villa on the outskirts of the village, placed on the same street as the church. He informed Pellat that he knew of nobody by that name, nor had he ever encountered any woman by the name of Anna Collumb, suggesting to her that perhaps she had been given an incorrect address. Gambais was a sleepy little village which had never had any trouble in all the centuries that it had stood, and the mayor had no intention of bringing trouble down on it when it was all the more likely that he had simply misunderstood the young woman's description of her Mr Cuchet.

In the neighbourhood by the Pére Lachaise cemetery in Paris, Annette Pascal was a well-known figure. A dressmaker for a famed fashion house, she had earned the dubious honour of being nicknamed "Madame Sombrero" due to the wide-brimmed hats that she liked to wear. She had divorced her husband after the death of their only child in infancy and now lived entirely alone. The work that she undertook was surprisingly arduous, with every success in design that she accomplished only leading her to have more work heaped upon her, and by the time that she came upon Henri's lonely-hearts advertisement in La Presse; Paris' leading evening newspaper, she was more than ready to escape from the life that she had spent so long building. She confided in some friends before going to meet with Henri, known to her as Mr Frémyet, that she was not so much interested in seeking a husband and partner but more enamoured with the idea of securing a *vieux monsieur*, what we would now refer to as a sugar daddy.

Mr Frémyet seemed to tick all the boxes as far as that went. He was a wealthy businessman from the south of France who seemed markedly more interested in the carnal aspects of marriage than was entirely proper. When Annette suggested that they need not marry at all if he was not completely devoted to the idea, he should have acted appalled, but in truth, it was more or less exactly what he had hoped to hear. They had an off-and-on affair that stretched out for almost two years until finally, he asked her to come with him to his villa in the country where he could take care of her properly. She departed Paris with him in April 1918 and was never seen again.

The Last Act

The First World War drew to a close in the same year that Henri murdered Annette Pascal, just a few months after he'd scattered her in his garden. The aftermath of the war saw a sudden influx of soldiers returning from the front, throwing France into chaos once more as it tried to accommodate the many walking wounded, and those who had been so traumatised by what came to be known as shell shock, who could no longer fully function. Chaos such as this was where Henri thrived. Men may have been returning, but they were returning to an unfamiliar world that he had been roaming freely for years. There may now have been some competition for the attention of women, but Henri had refined his pattern to a fine art by now.

Madam Marchadier was his final known victim. While she had lived throughout the war as a prostitute, she was now back in Paris working as a seamstress and hoarding her ever-dwindling reserves of cash. Henri met her through an attempt to sell off some of her more expensive furnishings, and soon won her confidence, inviting her, and her two beloved dogs, to live in Gambais with him.

He killed her and then strangled the dogs in precisely the same way. Butchering and burning their bodies in the same manner that he'd disposed of their owner. It was hardly the first time that he had killed an animal. The bones of several cats that had the temerity to bother him merely by their presence were already buried in his garden.

At about this time, Henri took an old leatherbound notebook that he had purchased many years before and had been gradually filling with notes, and he jotted down the names of the eleven people that he would eventually be convicted of murdering. Jotting them down in sequential order, based on the date of their death. He had hundreds of other names in the same notebook, hundreds of women that may also have been his victims, but they were never connected to him, never even looked into after his capture. It was simply too great a volume of work for the already taxed police to handle.

So too was tracking down and arresting a mass murderer. Despite the various missing person reports that they had received, all with the commonality of a description of Henri Landru in his various guises, the police had not begun to investigate a single one. There was only a single officer covering Gambais and its surrounding area, and he was in his late seventies and rarely left the station.

Until now, Marie Lacoste had ceased her investigation into Georges Frémyet. Perhaps she was working off the assumption that her half-sister was likely in league with the man or was so embarrassed to have been taken in by a con artist that she wanted to remain unnoticed. Marie most likely would have left things there, except for the sudden change that the end of the war had brought to her personal life.

Célestine's son had returned from the front lines now that the war was over, and he was blind. Shrapnel had brutalised his face, destroying his eyes, and leaving him at the mercy of the kindness of strangers. He had reached out to his mother for support, either physical or financial, and received no answer.

It was one matter for Célestine to ignore her half-sister out of shame, but her own son? It was a step too far. Marie Lacoste set about tracking Célestine down with the intent to drag her back to Paris, kicking and screaming, if necessary.

She presented the Parisian police with all of the information she had on Frémyet and his crimes, even positing the possibility that he had murdered her half-sister and attempted to do the same to her with his repeated invitations to meet him in secluded places. The police did the bare minimum of due diligence, visiting Célestine's old apartment and finding it bare, and unoccupied since 1917 before passing the buck. They informed Marie that if her sister had gone missing in Gambais, it was to Gambais and their attendant gendarmes that she would need to reach out for an investigation to be moved forward.

Needless to say, she was less than impressed, but she made an attempt to drive forward all the same, hastily scribing a letter to the mayor of Gambais, perfectly describing Henri and her half-sister, along with the precise address that he lived in the village and those few aliases of his that she had managed to uncover in her own investigations into the fraudster.

The mayor could not deny the oddity of the two letters that he had received in rapid succession, but he still did not intend to deal with anything untoward happening on his watch, so instead of providing Marie Lacoste with anything substantive about her missing half-sister, who nobody in Gambais had ever heard of, he put her in contact with Victorine Pellat.

The two women, realising that something was seriously wrong, pooled all of their information about Henri Landru, creating a dossier that would all but guarantee his arrest on suspicion of murder and handed it over to the police in the desperate hope that they might do something, anything, to prevent him from striking again.

The police did nothing with this information.

Lacoste and Pellat filed reports with the prosecutor's office in the department of Seine-et-Oise where Gambais was located, and it seemed briefly that something might actually be done, but the buck was passed once more, back to the very same officer that they had handed their dossier to, Inspector Jules Belin of the Paris Brigade Mobile.

Belin retyped some sections of the dossier, then filed it as his own report, while making no effort whatsoever to track down Henri Landru.

In fact, it would only be in April of 1919 that Henri was spotted in Paris again. A maid friend of Lacoste, who had seen Henri during one of his attempts to persuade Marie to accompany him for dinner, was out with her mistress on the Rue de Rivoli when she spotted him in a crockery shop with his latest girlfriend. She attempted to follow him but soon became fearful that he had recognised her, so she was forced to flee to the nearest police station.

Finally, Inspector Belin toddled into action. With an arrest warrant for Georges Frémyet in hand, he wandered into the crockery shop where Henri had been seen and retrieved his business card, following it to 76 Rue de Rochechouart, by the Gare de Nord, where he saw the lights on.

The murderer was in his sights, but it was getting a little late, and Belin was quite tired. His paperwork wasn't really in order for this arrest, since the business card that Georges Frémyet had left behind him had the name Lucien Guillet on it, so he elected to go home for the night and come back the following day with an amended warrant.

In the twelve hours that Henri was unattended, he could have fled Paris once more. He could have killed the young woman that he was with. He could have done just about anything. But in the end, it turned out he had done nothing but drink and talk all night with a pretty young thing. He was quite hungover when Belin arrested him the next day at about midday.

From the moment that Henri was taken into custody, he was combative, argumentative, and evasive. He refused to confirm his real name, forcing the police to investigate all of the different personas that he'd occupied separately.

Evidence was found, over the course of a year, of his embezzlement of funds from the ten women listed in his little black book but this did not necessarily translate to murder. Searching his various properties in Paris and Gambais, a great many of their belongings were found, but none of these immediately pointed to murder. The only real proof that Henri had killed anyone at all was found in the gardens of his villa in Gambais, where burnt and blackened fragments of bone were discovered under some leaves. They were too small to identify as human, let alone as belonging to his victims.

A report came in from the Gambais village doctor that Henri had been seen dumping a heavy sack into a local pond in the summer of 1916, but as this did not correlate to the timeline of the eleven murders noted in his little book, it was ignored by the police, and the pond left undisturbed.

Henri's whole family were dragged in for questioning once they had finally been found. Both of his sons now had criminal records of their own and were wise enough to deny any knowledge of anything to do with their father. Even when they were found to have belongings of the dead women, they claimed to have no knowledge of their provenance. Their mother, on the other hand, still had faith in the system and told the police everything that she knew, which amounted to very little when it came down to it. They were released without charges on the basis that they were no longer helping the investigation. The police had locked onto Henri as the sole perpetrator of all of his atrocities and meant for the full weight of punishment to land on him.

By this point, the case had been sensationalised in the Parisian newspapers beyond all reasonable measure, with the public in a frenzy over the idea that Paris had its very own sequential killer.

As such, when it came time for Henri to stand trial, it proved impossible to select a jury that had no knowledge of the case ahead of time. The case proceeded regardless. All of the evidence that had been gathered about Henri's finances were laid out to the jury as if they were damning evidence that he was a killer, rather than a simple confidence trickster.

Henri's defence lawyer was a staunch death-penalty abolitionist and one of the finest trial lawyers in all of France. He entered the courtroom in Versailles with almost as much aplomb and celebrity as his client. Vincent de Moro Giafferri expertly demolished every point that the prosecution made but was just as often undermined by Henri speaking out of turn, making odd pronouncements about the pacts that he'd made with the missing women to keep their secrets. Henri insisted that he was entirely innocent of all wrongdoing even as Moro tried to pull together a plea bargain for him, admitting to his crimes but commuting his sentence to transportation rather than execution.

The trial was the event of the season, with many celebrities attending and having their photographs taken in front of Henri Landru, the "Bluebeard of Gambais."

By the time that the jury returned a verdict, it had become apparent that things were not going to be straightforward. While they unanimously agreed that Henri had committed the acts of theft and fraud that he was accused of, they were split nine to three in favour of his guilt regarding the murder. It was considered not-proven by many of the jurors, even the ones who had voted for Henri's guilt. And matters were confused even further when Moro immediately approached the jurors to sign a letter requesting clemency for his client to avoid the death penalty.

Unfortunately, while all of the jurors were happy to sign it, Henri himself refused. He was not guilty. He had not done any of the things he was accused of. To admit that he was guilty would be to invite punishment, not protect him from it. He would not sign. He would appeal.

Mere days before his scheduled execution in 1922, Henri was finally convinced by Moro to sign the request for clemency, but it was immediately rejected by President Alexandre Millerand. For his crimes against the people of France, Henri had to die.

His final request, before he was taken out to be executed in front of the Prison Saint-Pierre in Versailles was for a footbath. He seemed to take great pleasure in receiving this last indulgence before making his walk out to the guillotine. He made no final statement, traversing the distance from the prison doors to the machinery in less than twenty seconds before his resolve could break.

From there his body was interred in a marked grave in the nearby Cimetière des Gonards for a period of five years, but when his family refused to pay rent on the plot, he was exhumed and reburied in an unmarked grave. Though not before some enterprising soul acquired his severed head to sell as a trophy. The head eventually found its way to the Museum of Death in Hollywood California, where you can still visit it to this day.

In the 1930s there was still a substantial tourist trade in Gambais off the back of Henri Landru's legend, and the villa in which he had committed his crimes was converted into a private restaurant which traded on his notoriety.

The oven, in which he had destroyed the remains of his victims, had been removed before the conversion into a restaurant, thankfully. It was sold to a private collector who meant to display it in Turin, Italy, beyond French law which prohibits such things. Unfortunately for this businessman, it seemed that Turin also had a sense of right and wrong, and declined to host his exhibit, resulting in the oven being sold along once more.

A hand-drawn picture of the oven was discovered in Moro's notes by his daughter after he had passed away. It had been made by Henri himself during the trial, and beside it, Henri had written "One can burn anything one wants in there."

In terms of criminology and psychology, Henri Landru is essentially unique. He is most assuredly a serial killer, but he defies classification in that he does not appear to follow any of the patterns that are usually recognisable in psychopaths. The model he most closely follows is that of the "black widow" style of serial killer. Even this classification, however, falls short because "black widow" killers are women who kill multiple men over an extended period of time for financial gain. Henri was a man killing women and while he did enjoy some financial gains, he also often subsidized the lifestyles of his victims, even if only temporarily.

Killing clearly satisfied some need in Henri but given how calmly and logically he addressed every problem that he encountered in his life, it seems most likely that the only need that it could have satisfied was the one for closure. He used murder to tie off loose threads so that he would no longer have to worry about them.

Given that one of the loose threads in his murder spree, Marie Lacoste, had eventually become the noose by which he was hanged, it seemed that killing was a sensible compulsion for him to follow. If there was any compulsion involved at all.

Even one hundred years later, it is impossible to fully quantify who Henri Landru was, and why he did what he did. There was no psychosexual component to his killings that can be found, nor any real financial gains that he couldn't have made considerably more easily by pursuing far easier methods of fraud. He had killed simply because he wanted the women he was dealing with to no longer exist when he was done with them.

Henri Landru was so egocentric that the women in his life were not people to him – nobody was a real person, except for Henri himself. He divorced himself from all sense of morality when it ceased to benefit him to toe the line of right and wrong. He killed over and over again, so that when he was finished playing with his toys, nobody else could pick them up, and more importantly, so that he would not get in trouble for breaking them.

Throughout history, there has never been another known case like the Landru "Bluebeard" murders, and it is for that reason that even after all of this time, he is still remembered as a unique monster

Every Review Helps

If you enjoyed the book and have a moment to spare, I would really appreciate a short review on Amazon. Your help in spreading the word is gratefully received and reviews make a huge difference to helping new readers find me. Without reviewers, us self-published authors would have a hard time!

Type in your link below to be taken straight to my book review page.

US	geni.us/shUS
UK	geni.us/shUK
Australia	geni.us/shAUS
Canada	geni.us/shCA

Thank you! I can't wait to read your thoughts.

About Ryan Green

Ryan Green is a true crime author who lives in Herefordshire, England with his wife, three children, and two dogs. Outside of writing and spending time with his family, Ryan enjoys walking, reading and windsurfing.

Ryan is fascinated with History, Psychology and True Crime. In 2015, he finally started researching and writing his own work and at the end of the year, he released his first book on Britain's most notorious serial killer, Harold Shipman.

He has since written several books on lesser-known subjects, and taken the unique approach of writing from the killer's perspective. He narrates some of the most chilling scenes you'll encounter in the True Crime genre.

You can sign up to Ryan's newsletter to receive a free book, updates, and the latest releases at:

WWW.RYANGREENBOOKS.COM

More Books by Ryan Green

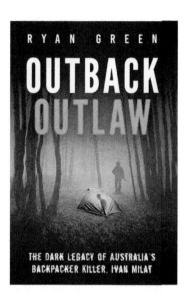

"He was going to kill somebody from the age of 10. It was built into him... I knew he was on a one-way trip. I knew that it was just a matter of how long." - Boris Milat, Ivan's brother

Detaining a man like Ivan Milat would be a monumental challenge. His obsession with firearms and hatred of state power were a highly volatile combination. Sending just a couple of men would result in two dead officers and a prime suspect on the run.

Outback Outlaw is an unflinching and uncompromising account of a man forever cemented in the annals of Australian true crime. Ryan Green's riveting narrative draws the reader into the real-life horror experienced by the victim and has all the elements of a classic thriller.

More Books by Ryan Green

On the bloodstained floor lay an array of butcher's tools and a body without a throat, torn out by Fritz's "love bite"...

Deemed psychologically unfit to stand trial for child abuse, Fritz Haarmann was locked up in a mental asylum until a new diagnosis as "morally inferior" allowed him to walk free. His insights into the criminal underworld convinced the police to overlook his "activities" and trust him as an informant.

What harm could it do?

When the dismembered and ravaged remains of young men began to wash up on the banks of the river, a war-torn nation cowered under the threat of the man known as the Butcher, Vampire and Wolf Man.
The hunt for the killer was on, and he was hiding in plain sight.

More Books by Ryan Green

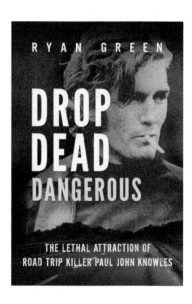

In 1974, the US East Coast was whipped up into a frenzy of fear. Locking their windows and doors, everyone was terrified of becoming the next victim of the strikingly handsome but deadly *"Casanova Killer"*. And he was on the move.

After being released from jail and promptly abandoned by his fiancée, Paul John Knowles embarked on a spate of gruesome murders on a road trip up the Pacific Coast.

No room for fear, no room for guilt, just the road

As the man-hunt gathered pace, the cold-blooded killing spree continued to defy detectives. With no visible pattern in the age, race nor gender of the victims, Knowle's joyride of kidnap, rape and murder tore across multiple state borders. It became a race of tragically high stakes. How many more lives would be lost before the police finally caught up.

More Books by Ryan Green

In 1861, the police of a rural French village tore their way into the woodside home of Martin Dumollard. Inside, they found chaos. Paths had been carved through mounds of bloodstained clothing, reaching as high as the ceiling in some places.

The officers assumed that the mysterious maid-robber had killed one woman but failed in his other attempts. Yet, it was becoming sickeningly clear that there was a vast gulf between the crimes they were aware of and the ones that had truly been committed.

Would Dumollard's wife expose his dark secret or was she inextricably linked to the atrocities? Whatever the circumstances, everyone was desperate to discover whether the bloody garments belonged to some of the 648 missing women.

More Books by Ryan Green

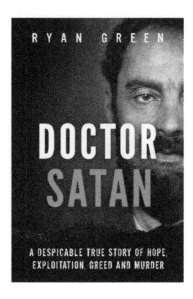

In 1944, as the Nazis occupied Paris, the French Police and Fire Brigade were called to investigate a vile-smelling smoke pouring out from a Parisian home. Inside, they were confronted with a scene from a nightmare. They found a factory line of bodies and multiple furnaces stocked with human remains. This was more than mere murder .

The homeowner was Dr. Marcel Petiot, an admired and charismatic physician. When questioned, Dr. Petiot claimed that he was a part of the Resistance and the bodies they discovered belonged to Nazi collaborators that he killed for the cause. The French Police, resentful of Nazi occupation and confused by a rational alternative, allowed him to leave.

Was the respected Doctor a clandestine hero fighting for national liberty or a deviant using dire domestic circumstances to his advantage? One thing is for certain, the Police and the Nazis both wanted to get their hands on Dr. Marcel Petiot to find out the truth.

Free True Crime Audiobook

Listen to four chilling True Crime stories in one collection. Follow the link below to download a FREE copy of *The Ryan Green True Crime Collection: Vol. 3.*

WWW.RYANGREENBOOKS.COM/FREE-AUDIOBOOK

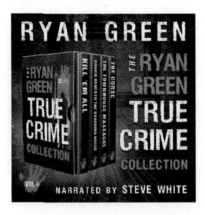

"Ryan Green has produced another excellent book and belongs at the top with true crime writers such as M. William Phelps, Gregg Olsen and Ann Rule" –**B.S. Reid**

"Wow! Chilling, shocking and totally riveting! I'm not going to sleep well after listening to this but the narration was fantastic. Crazy story but highly recommend for any true crime lover!" –**Mandy**

"Torture Mom by Ryan Green left me pretty speechless. The fact that it's a true story is just...wow" –**JStep**

"Graphic, upsetting, but superbly read and written" –**Ray C**

WWW.RYANGREENBOOKS.COM/FREE-AUDIOBOOK

Printed in Great Britain
by Amazon